GUADALCANAL

The naval conflict that now followed, in the waters around or within the Solomons island chain, has no parallel in the history of warfare – for its duration (there were actions almost daily over a period of some six months); for its ferocity, intensified by the fact that so many battles were fought by night, at very close quarters, in areas where lack of sea room left little space for manoeuvre; and for the almost continuous slaughter of ships and men.

– Ronald Lewin : *The Other Ultra*

By the same author:

Hurricane
The Battle of Leyte Gulf

GUADALCANAL

World War II's Fiercest Naval Campaign

ADRIAN STEWART

WILLIAM KIMBER · LONDON

First published in 1985 by
WILLIAM KIMBER & CO. LIMITED
100 Jermyn Street, London, SW1Y 6EE

© Adrian Stewart, 1985

ISBN 0-7183-0569-8

Typeset by Grove Graphics, Tring
and printed and bound in Great Britain by
The Garden City Press Limited,
Letchworth, Hertfordshire, SG6 1JS

To my Father
As Promised

Contents

List of Maps

List of Illustrations

*Unless otherwise credited, photographs are reproduced
by courtesy of US National Archives, Washington*

CHAPTER ONE

Invasion

A South Pacific island! The words conjure up such romantic visions: cloudless skies, blue waters, golden sands, vivid flowers, luscious fruits – a tropical paradise.

Reality is different. Reality is an island approximately ninety miles long by twenty-five miles wide, rising to 8,000 feet at its highest point. Rainfall is almost incessant throughout the year, though at its very worst from November to March. The island is covered with dense jungle, broken only by vile swamps or expanses of razor-sharp, seven-foot-tall kunai grass. Huge trees, with boles up to eight feet in diameter, rear well over a hundred feet high. Beneath them spreads an almost impenetrable maze of parasitical plants. Underfoot everywhere is thick, black, glutinous mud. The only signs of man's presence are some coconut plantations near the coast from which a few trails lead inland to clusters of dismal, filthy huts in dismal, filthy clearings; but all the most loathsome forms of life abound : enormous crocodiles, lizards, leeches, centipedes, scorpions, snakes, ants with incredibly vicious bites, spiders of nightmarish appearance, wasps three inches long, above all the lethal, malarial mosquitoes. Even the surrounding seas are grey and infested with sharks, while over them drifts the sickening stench of rotting vegetation.

Such is Guadalcanal in the Solomons group – a tropical hell.

The smell of death is only too appropriate, for in the summer and autumn of 1942, the navies of the United States of America and the Empire of Japan fought six major battles as well as scores of smaller actions around and for this accursed island. Savo Sound to the north of it, scene of four of the main actions, was re-christened Ironbottom Sound by the Americans from the numbers of sunken vessels that carpeted the sea bed. Professor S. E. Morison in the official *History of*

*United States Naval Operations in World War II** describes it simply
but accurately as an 'ocean graveyard'.

That anyone should want to fight for such a foul prize might seem
astounding, since to its unpleasantness must be added its remoteness.
The Solomon islands stretch for about 600 miles south-eastwards from
New Britain and New Ireland, which in turn lie to the east of New
Guinea. At the north-western end of the group is the island of Buka.
Then comes the largest, Bougainville. Next the Solomons separate,
forming a double chain divided by a deep, wide channel which the
Americans named 'The Slot'. The more northerly branch consists of
Choiseul, Santa Isabel, Florida and Malaita; the more southerly of
Shortland, Vella Lavella, Kolombangara, New Georgia, the Russell
Islands, Guadalcanal and San Christobal. At its nearest points, the
group lies some 800 miles north-east of Australia, some 1,800 miles
north-north-west of New Zealand.

Nor had the adversaries previously paid much attention to the
Solomons in general or Guadalcanal in particular. The United States
Marine Corps had collected information on almost every group of
Pacific islands except the Solomons. Major-General Alexander Vandegrift, who was ordered to command the invasion of Guadalcanal which
would mark the start of the most ferocious campaign in history, has
admitted that he had not hitherto known where Guadalcanal was.
His staff officers were forced to draw up their operational plans on the
basis of maps which turned out to be not only inaccurate but in-
complete – they showed the course of rivers, for instance, only by
dotted lines.

The Japanese displayed greater interest in and certainly possessed
greater knowledge of the area as a whole. As far back as September
1941, the staff of Vice-Admiral Inouye's Fourth Fleet had urged that
positions in the Solomons be occupied in the event of hostilities. When
these took place, the Japanese on 23rd January 1942, seized Kavieng
on New Ireland and the splendid natural harbour of Rabaul on New
Britain, which they built up into their main southern base. During
March and April they also landed on Buka, Bougainville and Shortland, while on 3rd May, they occupied and later set up a seaplane
base at Tulagi, a small island sheltered by a large bay to the south of

* Volume V: *The Struggle for Guadalcanal August 1942–February 1943.*

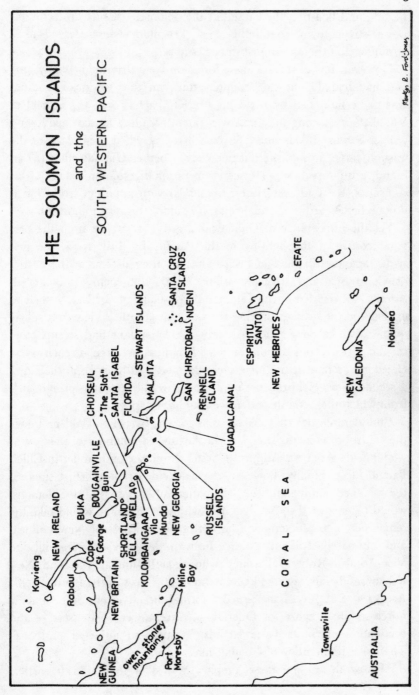

THE SOLOMON ISLANDS
and the
SOUTH WESTERN PACIFIC

Marjory R. Ford-Jones

Florida and boasting the capital of the Solomon Islands Protectorate; a one-street town containing a cricket-pitch, which served as a reminder that these were British possessions.

However, few of the Japanese forces on New Britain knew anything of Guadalcanal. The first counter-attack on the American landings was to be launched by the 25th Air Flotilla based at the airfield of Vunakanau. Among the pilots was Japan's leading fighter 'ace', Petty Officer Saburo Sakai, who later recorded that when the orders for the mission came through he did not know whether Guadalcanal was an island, a military base, or a secret operational code-name. One of his comrades, Petty Officer Hatori, remarked with apparent truth that if no one had heard of Guadalcanal, it couldn't be very important.

Yet the importance of Guadalcanal arose inevitably from the previous course of the fighting in the Pacific. By July 1942, the first swift Japanese thrusts had been halted by their defeats at the Battles of Coral Sea and Midway Island. With the enemy unbalanced, Admiral Ernest King, the Commander-in-Chief, US Fleet, wished to exploit success by re-capturing the Solomons, with a view to a subsequent advance on Rabaul. Already the Americans had set up bases in the Fijis, Tongatabu, Samoa, Noumea in Free French New Caledonia, Efate in the New Hebrides and finally in Espiritu Santo, a second New Hebrides position. These would serve as springboards from which their counter-offensive could develop.

Considerable debate took place as to whether this would be under the control of General Douglas MacArthur, commander of the Southwest Pacific Area, or Admiral Chester Nimitz, Commander-in-Chief, Pacific Fleet. Finally, however, it was decided that the first stage of the planned campaign, the occupation of the southern Solomons, would be entrusted to Nimitz, after which MacArthur would take the remainder of the Solomons, the north-eastern coast of New Guinea, and ultimately Rabaul. Nimitz in turn delegated responsibility to Vice-Admiral Robert Ghormley, who on 18th June at Auckland, New Zealand, officially assumed command of all forces in the South Pacific Area. On 2nd July, King issued a formal directive that South Pacific Force should prepare for Operation 'Watchtower' – the 'seizure and occupation of Santa Cruz Islands, Tulagi and adjacent positions'. There was no mention of Guadalcanal.

Meanwhile the Japanese, despite the loss of four aircraft carriers at Midway, were by no means downhearted. It had never been their intention to conquer America, a task for which they were well aware that their resources were utterly inadequate. Instead they proposed first to take the Philippines, Malaya and the Dutch East Indies in order to secure the raw materials, chiefly oil, rubber and tin, which their country lacked; then to build up around them a defensive barrier of such strength that their enemies could be persuaded to negotiate a compromise peace, leaving Japan with at least the bulk of her conquests, in preference to fighting a costly war of indefinite duration.

Indeed the Army section of Imperial General Headquarters had concluded that the time for consolidation had come by the end of April 1942, but the Naval Commander-in-Chief, Admiral Isoroku Yamamoto, insisted on further offensives in the hope of annihilating the US fleet in a 'decisive battle' – another Trafalgar or Tsushima. After the disaster at Midway, however, Yamamoto too was forced to agree that priority must be given to strengthening the defensive perimeter. Furthermore he recognized that Japan's newly-won empire – which went by the pompous title of the 'Greater East Asia Co-Prosperity Sphere' – was at its most vulnerable at the south-eastern extremity – the Solomon Islands.

A new Eighth Fleet was therefore created at Rabaul under the command of Vice-Admiral Gunichi Mikawa. More aircraft poured into north-eastern New Guinea, New Britain and the northern Solomons. And it was decided that the Japanese Army would eliminate the threat to Rabaul posed by the Allied base at Port Moresby on the southern coast of New Guinea by an advance over the Owen Stanley mountains. To protect the flank of this movement, airfields would be needed in the southern Solomons. On 28th May, a patrol from Tulagi had landed on Guadalcanal, though only to machine-gun some unfortunate cattle for meat. Yet it must have been a report from this or a similar landing later which indicated that the flat coconut grove at Lunga Plain on the north of the island would make a promising site for an aerodrome.

Thus Guadalcanal entered the strategic picture with a vengeance. An airfield there would dominate the entire area, threatening the whole American position in the South Pacific. If the Japanese could complete it undetected, Operation 'Watchtower' would be doomed.

Luckily the Americans were kept well informed of their foes' plans. As is now well known they had broken the main Japanese naval code (which they called JN25) but this was changed at intervals and when this happened, as it did both in late May and in late July 1942, some time inevitably elapsed before the cryptanalysts could again read enemy signals. 'Traffic analysis', which is a study of call signs and the changing volume of signals, could give valuable clues, but most information came from the oldest source of all.

When details of the Japanese plans for their assault on Midway, which had in fact been gleaned by the code-breakers, were distributed to the American naval officers who would defend the island, one was heard to mutter : 'That man of ours in Tokyo is worth every cent we pay him'. There was no 'agent' in Tokyo, but there were quite a number throughout the Solomons.

They went by the unromantic name of 'coastwatchers'. Organized by Australian Commander Eric Feldt, they were traders, planters or colonial officials, volunteers all, who either remained in the islands after the Japanese occupation or were brought back there later by US ships or aircraft. Equipped with a durable, efficient 'teleradio' – a transmitter, receiver and generator – and aided by trusted natives, whose loyalty was beyond praise, these devoted spies were, says Morison, 'of inestimable value throughout the Solomons campaign'. Many of them, alas, were detected and met lonely deaths.

The most distinguished British resident to take to the jungle when the Japanese arrived was the Right Reverend Walter Baddeley, Anglican Bishop of Melanesia, but perhaps the most important was an officer called Captain Martin Clemens, who just before the occupation of Tulagi, had moved to Guadalcanal, whence, aided by two Australians named Rhoades and Macfarlan and a small group of native assistants, he sent in regular reports of enemy activity.

On 19th June, Clemens signalled the first ominous piece of news : the Japanese had made a survey of the Lunga plantation. By the end of the month, there were over 2,500 Japanese on Guadalcanal, hard at work downing the coconut trees to make room for their planned airfield. Clemens continued sending his alarming messages, which were confirmed by an American reconnaissance flight over the island on 4th July. Admiral King hesitated no longer : he issued orders

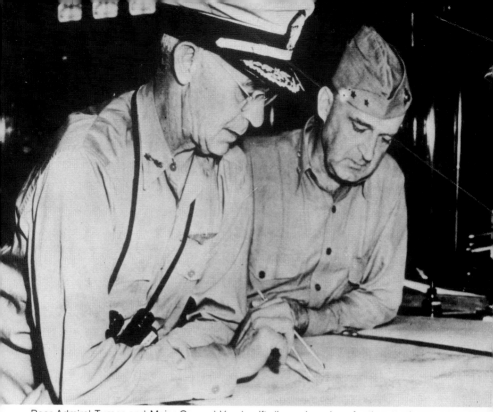

Rear-Admiral Turner and Major-General Vandegrift discussing plans for the attack on Guadalcanal.

American forces landing on Guadalcanal.

American forces crossing a river on Guadalcanal by means of a ferry-boat prepared by Marine Engineers.

that 'Watchtower' must include a landing on Guadalcanal and must commence on 1st August.

The force detailed to take Guadalcanal – which was code-named 'Cactus' – as well as Tulagi, was Major-General Alexander Vandegrift's First Marine Division. Its first echelon, including the Headquarters Staff, reached Wellington on 14th June. The remainder, less one regiment previously sent to garrison Samoa, was due to arrive on 11th July. Although the division had a hard core of veterans, thousands of its men were new recruits, still only partly trained. Many of its units had had no experience of amphibious operations or even amphibious manoeuvres. However, Vandegrift was unconcerned since he had been told that his command need not expect combat before January 1943, which would give him plenty of time to remedy deficiencies.

His consternation may well be imagined therefore, when at a conference at Auckland to which he was summoned by Ghormley on 25th June, he learned of the task before him. Even though 'D-Day' was later postponed to 7th August, time was desperately short.

Vandegrift's first duty was to unload his transports, including those of his second echelon when this arrived, in order to reload 'combat style'. This means stowing equipment so that those items most urgently needed on a beach-head could be landed first, followed by less necessary ones in a complicated system of priorities. Such a method wastes a great deal of space. Almost all personal cargo had therefore to be omitted, while supplies of food, fuel, even ammunition, were much reduced, leaving the landing force with only enough to enable it to live and fight.

To add to the Americans' misery, driving winter rains now fell upon Wellington. Thereupon the New Zealand dockers, regarding trade union rules as more important than anything else, refused to work during 'inclement' weather. The Marines had to load their transports unaided, while the storms burst open cardboard containers, reducing the quay to a sodden swamp of cigarette cartons, cornflakes and socks.

Yet somehow the task was completed. On 22nd July, an indignant, exhausted division left Wellington for the Fijis, where it was joined by another convoy carrying a regiment of Second Marine Division, a raider battalion, a defence battalion* and a parachute battalion (minus parachutes), the whole being designated the First Marine Division, Reinforced.

The troops were carried in nineteen transports backed up by four converted destroyers, *Colhoun, Little, Gregory* and *McKean*, the first three of which would not survive the campaign. Transport *McCawley* flew the flag of Rear-Admiral Richmond Kelly Turner, an able, energetic but irascible officer who was in charge of the amphibious forces and to whom Vandegrift was subordinate. So also was Rear-Admiral Victor Crutchley RN, a jovial, red-bearded figure, who had won a VC during the gallant though unsuccessful attempt to block the Ostend entrance to the Bruges Canal on 9/10th May 1918. Crutchley commanded the escorting naval vessels : six heavy cruisers : HMAS *Australia* (his flagship) and *Canberra*, and USS *Chicago*, *Vincennes, Quincy* and *Astoria*; two light cruisers : USS *San Juan* and HMAS *Hobart*; fifteen destroyers (all American) : *Selfridge*, *Patterson, Ralph Talbot, Mugford, Jarvis, Blue, Helm, Henley*, *Bagley, Hull, Dewey, Ellet, Wilson, Monssen* and *Buchanan*; and five minesweepers.

Additional aid would come from the land-based aircraft of Mac-Arthur's Air Commander, General George Kenney, and Ghormley's Air Commander, Rear-Admiral John McCain. So great, however, were the distances involved, that apart from reconnaissance aircraft only B-17 Flying Fortresses could reach the southern Solomons, while it was quite out of the question for Kenney or McCain to provide either close support or fighter cover.

Consequently, Turner's Task Force 62 rendezvoused in the Fijis with Vice-Admiral Frank Jack Fletcher's Task Force 61. On the decks of fleet carriers *Saratoga, Enterprise* and *Wasp* were clustered 99 Wildcat fighters, 103 Dauntless dive-bombers and 41 of the splendidly adaptable Avengers which could be used for reconnaissance or as torpedo-bombers or glide-bombers as desired. Protecting the vital, vulnerable 'flat-tops' were battleship *North Carolina*, heavy cruisers *Minneapolis*, *New Orleans, Portland, San Francisco* and *Salt Lake City*, light cruiser *Atlanta* and destroyers *Phelps, Farragut, Worden, MacDonough*,

---

* A raider battalion was equivalent to a British commando unit. A defence battalion was a unit designed for island defence with a high ratio of firepower to manpower.

Dale, Balch, Maury, Gwin, Benham, Grayson, Lang, Sterett, Aaron Ward, Stack, Laffey and *Farenholt.*

Thus a very large proportion of the US Pacific Fleet had been allocated to 'Watchtower', including several recent arrivals from the Atlantic, among them *Wasp, North Carolina, Vincennes* and *Quincy.* Yet Vice-Admiral Ghormley, the nominal commander of this splendid force, was then en route to Noumea, where he proposed to set up his headquarters. He did not meet his chief officers to discuss operational plans but instead delegated responsibility, but gave no instructions, to Fletcher. Furthermore it seems that it was at no time made clear to Fletcher that he was in charge of all aspects of the coming mission which incidentally was of a type of which he had had no previous experience.

Unlike Ghormley whose most recent assignments had been staff positions, as Director of the War Plans Division in the office of the Chief of Naval Operations, or as special naval observer in London, Fletcher had seen a great deal of action, having commanded the American forces at the vital Battles of Coral Sea and Midway. He would not have been human had the strain of these tremendous responsibilities not taken its toll. After seeing carrier *Lexington* sunk in the former battle and carrier *Yorktown* in the latter, he had a healthy respect for Japanese naval-air power, which in turn made him understandably reluctant to risk further losses.

In consequence, when on the afternoon of 26th July, Turner, McCain, Vandegrift and his own chief subordinates Rear-Admirals Thomas Kinkaid and Leigh Noyes went aboard *Saratoga*, Fletcher abruptly announced that because of the danger of air attacks on his carriers, he neither could nor would keep Task Force 61 within striking range of Guadalcanal for more than two days. Both Turner and Vandegrift protested as strongly as possible that it would take four or five days to unload the transports, during which time air protection was essential. Fletcher merely retorted that if the landings could not be completed within two days they should not take place at all.

As already mentioned, Fletcher's superior officer Vice-Admiral Ghormley was not among those present, but his Chief of Staff had flown in from Noumea. This was Rear-Admiral Daniel Callaghan, whom Brigadier-General S. B. Griffith USMC in his book *The Battle for Guadalcanal* describes, somewhat unkindly, as 'a handsome and personable officer whose principal qualification for the demanding post he occupied was that he had been President Roosevelt's naval aide'. He raised no objection but merely 'took notes in silence'. Fletcher therefore, without further discussion, curtly closed the conference, 'if', says Griffith acidly, 'this gathering may accurately be so described'.

Rehearsals followed. Since a coral reef prevented most of the boats from landing, while supporting gunfire proved unreliable, as did covering air attacks, neither Turner nor Vandegrift can have gained much consolation from these. However, they did their best in the pitifully short time available, to apply the many lessons they had learned.

As if in recognition of their determination, fortune now began to smile on the Americans. While Fletcher's carriers manoeuvred some 100 miles south of Guadalcanal, the amphibious forces closed in under driving rain which shielded them from the prying eyes of enemy reconnaissance aircraft. Not until dawn on 7th August did the Japanese on Tulagi report the invasion shipping to the Eighth Fleet at Rabaul, with a query as to their identity. Seconds later at 0613 the query was answered by 8-inch shells from heavy cruiser *Quincy* as she began a bombardment of a suspected enemy strongpoint on Guadalcanal.

Under cover of naval gunfire and while strikes from carrier-planes wiped out the flying-boats and floatplane fighters* moored at the Japanese seaplane base, the Marines headed for the beaches. Those detailed for Guadalcanal under Vandegrift's direct command landed without resistance. They then began a slow, highly disorganized advance towards the airfield, which fortunately was opposed only by a few snipers, as the majority of the Japanese on the island were not fighting men but construction workers. In the mid-afternoon of 8th August, the Americans captured the landing-ground, which they named Henderson Field in honour of Major Lofton Henderson, a Marine flier killed at Midway.

Surprise was complete. Tractors, trucks, building materials, food supplies, cases of Japanese beer, a refrigeration plant, clothing, helmets, rifles; all fell into American hands. Even more valuable were

---

* These were specially-built variants of the Mitsubishi Zero. The type was code-named 'Rufe' by the Allies.

certain secret documents – including a code-book – salvaged from a smouldering bonfire on the edge of the airfield. A few days later, the Marines acquired a different source of information when coastwatcher Clemens entered their lines. True to British tradition, he emerged from the jungle, cool, poised and immaculately dressed.

In the meantime, there was little cool or poised about the situation on the beaches. Equipment of all sorts – rations, fuel, ammunition, medical supplies – piled up in ever-mounting disorder, providing dangerous targets for enemy aircraft, while scores of small boats hovered off-shore in confused groups, looking for a place where they could unload. On Vandegrift's suggestion, Turner began landing cargo on other beaches about a mile to the west, but even this did little to ease the problem.

Across Savo Sound, as it was then still named, Vandegrift's second-in-command, Brigadier-General Rupertus, was also meeting with difficulties. He had been ordered to take Tulagi together with the nearby islets of Gavutu and Tanambogo which were linked by a causeway, but in contrast to the easy progress on Guadalcanal, his troops were soon engaged in desperate combat. At 0630, Tulagi radioed : 'Enemy force overwhelming. We will defend our posts to the death'. The promise was not an idle one; the events of the 7th August gave warning to the Americans of what ferociously determined defensive fighters the Japanese could be.

The actual landing on Tulagi was easy, since the Americans had shrewdly chosen a seemingly unsuitable beach in the hope, which proved justified, that this would not be defended. The reduction of the island emphatically was not. 'Each Jap fought until he was killed', reported Vandegrift, 'each machine-gun crew to the last man, who almost invariably killed himself rather than surrender'. It was not until late evening of the following day, 8th August, that the outnumbered, out-gunned defenders were at last eliminated.

On Gavutu, the fighting was even more fierce. Although the islet measures only about 500 yards by less than 300 yards, the Japanese positions, sited in caves, were so well protected that neither air nor naval bombardment was able to inflict serious damage on them. Again the struggle lasted through until 8th August, organized resistance ceasing shortly after noon.

Tanambogo, smallest of the targets, proved the toughest of all.

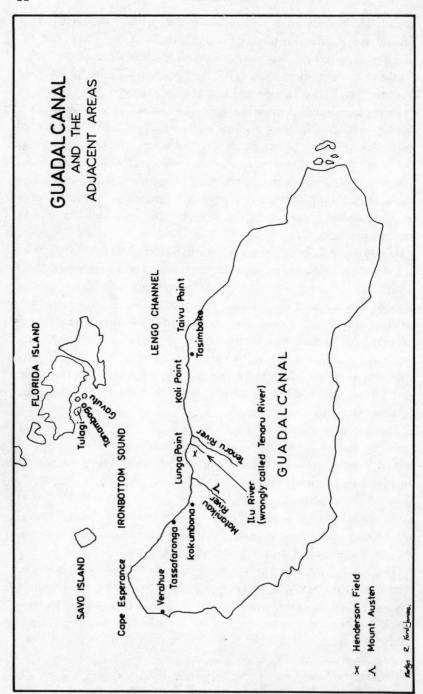

Even after Gavutu was secured, its resolute garrison, which had already repulsed an attempted landing on the previous night, kept the Americans back from the connecting causeway.

Assistance was clearly necessary. A dive-bomber attack was ordered against Tanambogo but the bombs fell short, killing three Marines on Gavutu, wounding nine others. Then light cruiser *San Juan* shelled the defences, only to suffer an accidental turret explosion which added five dead and thirteen wounded to the American losses. Next came another air-strike which again hit the wrong island causing further casualties, three more of them fatal. Finally at 1600, destroyer *Buchanan*, steaming boldly close inshore, delivered a highly effective bombardment which enabled the Marines to land five minutes later.

Yet for a further day the defenders continued a desperate resistance which may be symbolized by one incident. One of a pair of light tanks which had been brought ashore, moved too far ahead of its supporting troops. The Japanese rushed it, quite regardless of casualties – 42 bodies were later found piled up around it – stalled the track with an iron bar and set it on fire with oil-soaked rags, killing all the crew except one.

Finally by mid-afternoon of 9th August, Rupertus was able to inform Vandegrift that all objectives had been taken. The Americans had suffered 295 casualties, over 100 of them fatal.* The Japanese garrisons had been all but exterminated, though about 75 men had escaped by swimming to Florida island. Only 23, all of them wounded, were taken prisoner.

Nor had the Japanese any intention of allowing their foes to retain their hard-won gains. Admiral Yamamoto, on hearing the news, ordered that 'first priority' should be given to the recapture of Guadalcanal, while Vice-Admiral Mikawa at Rabaul was already putting in hand plans to land reinforcements on the island, mount a counter-attack by surface vessels and launch an air-strike.

The last-named was the most easy to carry into effect. At 0900 7th August, Rear-Admiral Sadayoshi Yamada, commanding the 25th Air Flotilla, directed 27 twin-engined Mitsubishi bombers – which the

* Also the strength of the defence had forced Rupertus to throw in all his reserves, with the result that the proposed landing on the Santa Cruz Islands was cancelled. However, since they are infested with malignant malaria, this may have been desirable rather than otherwise.

Americans knew as 'Bettys' – escorted by eighteen Zeros, against the landing-forces.* The Bettys had previously been armed with bombs in preparation for a raid on Port Moresby, but it was felt that no time could be lost re-equipping them with torpedoes which were much more deadly against ships – a decision which turned out to be a grave error.

It was compounded by a worse one. When the attackers reached Guadalcanal, they were presented with an ideal target for their bombs in the supplies scattered in plain sight all over the beaches. Yet now, as in a later strike that day, they concentrated entirely on the shipping. Thus, says Major Frank Hough in *The Island War*, they 'proceeded to ignore their main chance. . . . Had those supplies been destroyed or even seriously damaged, the expedition would have been doomed at a single stroke, as events were to prove.'

Nor did the raiders achieve surprise. Shortly after 1030, an Australian coastwatcher, Lieutenant Paul Mason, in his hide-out on the Bougainville hills saw them roar overhead. His warning signal had to cover a somewhat diverse path – to Port Moresby, to Townsville, Australia, to Canberra, to Pearl Harbor – before reaching Turner but that officer still had about an hour in which to ensure that his transports were manoeuvring at speed, screened by the warships, with a strong Combat Air Patrol (CAP) of Wildcats from *Saratoga* and *Enterprise* overhead, when radar located the enemy at about 1315. No damage was suffered by any American vessel.

Unhappily the air-combats were less satisfactory. The fighter-direction team in heavy cruiser *Chicago* proved inexperienced but the Wildcats, joined with splendid if foolhardy courage by some SBD Dauntless scout/dive-bombers from *Enterprise* and *Wasp*, were able to bring down four Bettys and two of their escorts. The Zeros which came from the highly skilled and experienced Tainan Air Group destroyed eight American fighters.

One Dauntless was also lost. The redoubtable Petty Officer Saburo Sakai, recovering from his astonishment at being attacked by a dive-

---

* The Allies avoided difficulties caused by the complicated Japanese system of aircraft classification, plus the problem of pronunciation, by giving each type an arbitrary code-name; the bombers having ladies' names; the fighters men's names. The exception was Mitsubishi's famous fighter which was almost always known as the Zero, or – to RAF pilots – the Navy Nought, not by its official code-name of 'Zeke'.

bomber, retaliated quickly. As he recounted in his book *Samurai* :

> I closed in rapidly and fired. The rear gunner flung up his hands
> and collapsed over his gun. I pulled back easily on the stick and
> the shells walked up to the engine. The SBD rolled repeatedly to
> the left, then dropped into a wild dive. Yonekawa* saw the pilot
> bale out. It was my sixtieth kill.

Only minutes later, Sakai was struck by machine-gun fire from the
gunner of another Dauntless. Terribly wounded in the head, permanently blinded in his right eye, he managed by a quite incredible
effort of will to bring his battered Zero all the way back to Rabaul,
landed safely, and collapsed from loss of blood. He recovered, flew
again, downed four more enemy aircraft, was promoted to ensign,
then to sub-lieutenant – the first non-commissioned Japanese airman
to become an officer other than as a posthumous honour – and survived the war. The fighting on Tulagi, Gavutu and Tanambogo had
already shown how determined Japanese resistance was likely to
prove. If the Americans had known of Sakai's exploit, they would
have been given a clearer warning still.

At about 1500, sixteen unescorted Val dive-bombers, which had
refuelled at Buka landing-field, launched a second strike. This time
the raiders achieved complete surprise yet they only managed to score
one hit, on destroyer *Mugford*, which did little damage though it
killed 22 of the crew. As the Vals pulled away, the Wildcats tore into
them. Although the resulting slaughter was not so great as the American airmen claimed, enemy records indicate that ten dive-bombers
were either shot down or so badly damaged that they failed to return
to base.

On 8th August, just before noon, Yamada's Bettys were back, now
armed with torpedoes. Japanese aircraft were not able to carry the
deadly 24-inch 'Long Lances' used by their cruisers and destroyers – a
fact which cannot be emphasised too strongly in view of the numerous
accounts which solemnly repeat that they could. In reality they had
17.7-inch weapons which admittedly were superior to those of the

---

* Petty Officer Yonekawa was Sakai's wingman.

Allies since they could be dropped from a safer, because greater, height and range.

Once again, an Australian coastwatcher on Bougainville, Lieutenant Jack Read, gave warning of the attack, but the twenty Bettys, coming in at low level, caught the American fighters, who expected another bombing raid, by surprise. Four Wildcats from *Enterprise* alone managed a successful interception, downing four torpedo-planes plus one of the 24 escorting Zeros. After the attack, a Dauntless from *Wasp* claimed another Betty. Apart from this, the only defence was the concentrated fire of Turner's AA gunners.

This, however, proved deadly. The Americans had spent much time practising tracking low-flying aircraft, their fire-control systems were good and the Betty, though in many ways an excellent machine, caught fire too easily. Only one torpedo found its mark in the bow of destroyer *Jarvis*, causing heavy but not fatal damage. Thirteen more torpedo-planes went blazing to their doom.

Yet in the middle of this disaster, the Japanese pilots gave a terrifying illustration of their implacable resolve. Two of them, fatally hit, tried to ram their targets. One of these suicide attackers disintegrated under anti-aircraft fire but the other crashed into transport *George F. Elliott* with a thunderous explosion. Burning petrol poured over her deck, part of her crew, it seems, abandoned ship prematurely and by the time darkness fell, the vessel was a blazing hulk which ultimately sank together with a large quantity of valuable supplies.

Despite her loss and the delays in unloading caused by the air attacks, Rear-Admiral Turner was probably not too dissatisfied with the position on the evening of 8th August, but at 1807, he intercepted a signal from Fletcher to Ghormley which shattered his composure. It read :

Fighter plane strength reduced from 99 to 78. In view of the large number of enemy torpedo-planes and bombers in this area, I recommend the immediate withdrawal of my carriers. Request tankers sent forward immediately as fuel running low.

Fletcher's decision, which Turner bluntly called 'desertion' and even Nimitz, always reluctant to criticize, thought 'most unfortunate' seems impossible to justify. Twenty-one Wildcats had been lost from various causes but, as Morison has pointed out, this still gave Fletcher one more than the American carriers had had at Midway. No enemy reconnaissance aircraft had yet attacked or even located Task Force 61. Post-war analysis has shown that there were no urgent problems of fuel shortage and if there had been, Fletcher, as Nimitz would suggest later, could have solved them by sending his carriers (plus supporting warships) southwards one at a time to rendezvous with the tankers. Furthermore, having sent off his signal, Fletcher did not wait for Ghormley's consent – which finally came through some twelve hours later – but initiated his withdrawal without delay.

There seems little doubt that the real cause of Fletcher's retirement was his fear of Japanese air attacks. Similarly, on hearing the grim news, Turner's first thought was that he would now have no fighter protection. Yet, as it transpired, the crucial danger lay elsewhere. A major Japanese counter-attack was indeed imminent – but it would not come from the skies.

CHAPTER TWO

The Battle of Savo Island

Vice-Admiral Gunichi Mikawa, Commander, Eighth Fleet at Rabaul, was a reliable, resolute officer who had previously commanded the vessels which had screened Vice-Admiral Chuichi Nagumo's carriers during their triumphant progress from Pearl Harbor to the Indian Ocean – as well as at Midway Island where this had ended in shattering defeat. On hearing the news of the Guadalcanal landings, he promptly put in hand a variety of counter-measures, with differing results.

As previously related, Mikawa's air-attacks achieved little. His planned reinforcement of the Japanese garrison was even less successful. He hastily embarked the few troops available in some transports, which were ordered to sail to the island. At this time, however, so many Japanese convoys were at sea that Mikawa could not provide his expedition with an adequate destroyer escort. At midnight on 8th August, while it was passing some fourteen miles west of Cape St George, New Ireland, it was sighted by US submarine *S-38*. Two torpedoes struck the largest transport, the 5,600-ton *Meiyo Maru*, which went to the bottom with 14 officers and 328 men. Her loss caused Mikawa to recall her companions to Rabaul.

There remained Mikawa's proposed surface attack. A hurried signal was made, ordering the five heavy cruisers of Rear-Admiral Aritomo Goto at Kavieng to proceed at once to Rabaul. One of these, *Chokai*, entered the harbour, where Mikawa boarded her, broke out his red and white striped flag and headed for Buka Island, followed by the other four, *Aoba* (Goto's flagship), *Kako*, *Kinugasa* and *Furutaka*, plus light cruisers *Tenryu* and *Yubari* from Rabaul and a solitary destroyer, *Yunagi*, from Kavieng.

Through the night of 7/8th August, Mikawa led his ships north of

28

Buka, then at 0200, turned south-east to cruise along the eastern shore of Bougainville. At 0625, all five heavy cruisers catapulted a seaplane to search ahead. By noon, the scouts were back. In the prevailing good weather they were able to land safely on the sea, whence they were hoisted onto their ships by derricks. Two of them had made a thorough reconnaissance over Guadalcanal and Tulagi, despite anti-aircraft fire and interference from American fighters which their experienced pilots had avoided by skilful use of cloud-cover. They reported the presence of one battleship, six cruisers, nineteen destroyers and eighteen transports.

The mention of that mythical battleship may have caused Mikawa some anxieties, but, since naturally he had no inkling of Fletcher's planned withdrawal, he was most concerned about possible attacks from American carrier aircraft, for which his experiences at Midway had given him a healthy respect. Nevertheless at about 1300, he ordered speed increased and entered the Slot* to race for Guadalcanal at 24 knots. Mikawa's battle-plan, as given to all his ships, was to arrive in the target area during the early hours of 9th August, overcome any opposition by Allied warships, then fall on the transports off Guadalcanal. After that he would repeat the process off Tulagi, finally returning in daylight up the Slot. He accepted the risk of air-attacks during his retirement. At 1840, as the sudden tropical darkness fell, he signalled : 'Let us attack with certain victory in the traditional night attack of the Imperial Navy.† May each one calmly do his utmost.'

Mikawa had good reason for confidence. The Japanese Navy had for years planned that in the event of hostilities it would offset its numerical inferiority by superiority in night-fighting. To this end, it had carried out exercises, regardless of risk, which by the time that war broke out had already made its seamen experts in such operations.

This was especially so with regard to the lookouts, who in ironical contrast to the pre-war propaganda that the Japanese suffered from poor night-vision, were specially selected and trained for their work. Equipped with huge, exceptionally powerful night binoculars, their ability and alertness alike were to prove outstanding.

* The Slot, it will be recalled, was the channel lying between the two main branches of the Solomon chain.
† This was a reference to the destroyer attack on Port Arthur with which Japan had begun her war with Russia on the night of 8/9th February 1904.

In addition the Japanese had developed highly reliable starshells and powerful searchlights, the control of which was linked to that of the ships' guns. Yet by far their most effective weapons were their 'Long Lance' torpedoes – fearful killers which, propelled by oxygen-enriched fuel, could carry a warhead twice the size of that of their American equivalents for 44,000 yards at 36 knots or for 22,000 yards at 49 knots.

Thus Mikawa's force provided a deadly threat which was made the greater because the Allies did not realize that it was imminent. As mentioned earlier, a change in the Japanese code had robbed the defenders of the advance information which had proved so decisive at Midway; there had, however, been a number of sightings that might have given warning of what lay ahead – if they had been interpreted correctly.

On 7th August at about 1230, B-17 Flying Fortresses of MacArthur's command sighted 'six unidentified ships' – which were in fact Goto's five heavy cruisers plus destroyer *Yunagi* – en route for Rabaul. Next as Mikawa's entire force left St George's Channel between New Britain and New Ireland at 2000, it was sighted by submarine *S-38*. Unfortunately on this occasion Lieutenant-Commander Munson, who was soon to sink *Meiyo Maru*, could not reach a good firing position. In the darkness also, he did not evaluate the enemy strength accurately, reporting it as 'two destroyers and three larger ships of unknown type'.

When news of these encounters reached Turner and Crutchley, neither felt much concern. The presence of not very powerful forces near to a major enemy base 550 miles from Guadalcanal appeared to have little significance. Munson had stated that the group he had sighted was moving 'at high speed' which did suggest it was on an urgent mission, but there was nothing to indicate that this was an attack on the landing-forces. Even if it should be, there seemed no immediate cause for alarm, since the vessels were bound to be spotted by reconnaissance aircraft on the following day.

And in fact at 1026, a RAAF Hudson from Milne Bay, New Guinea, did sight Mikawa's warriors. The Japanese had no fighter cover but they sent up heavy anti-aircraft fire which kept the 'snooper' at a distance. Unfortunately its pilot did not break radio silence to announce his find, as he had orders to do in an urgent case, but com-

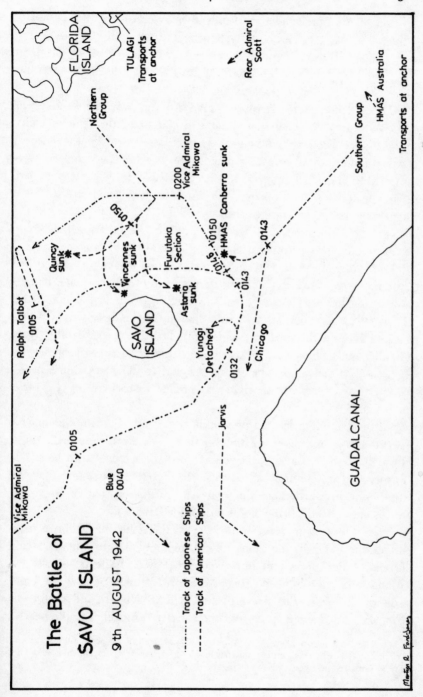

The Battle of
SAVO ISLAND

9th AUGUST 1942

········· Track of Japanese Ships
----- Track of American Ships

FLORIDA ISLAND

TULAGI
Transports at anchor

Rear Admiral Scott

Northern Group

Southern Group
HMAS Australia

Transports at anchor

0200
Vice Admiral Mikawa

0150

HMAS Canberra sunk

0143

Quincy sunk

Vincennes sunk

Furutaka Section

0150
0146

0143

0146

Astoria sunk

Chicago

Ralph Talbot 0105

SAVO ISLAND

Yunagi Detached

0132

Vice Admiral Mikawa

0105

Blue 0040

Jarvis

GUADALCANAL

Martin A. Ford-Jones

pleted his mission, landed and only then released his information. It did not reach Crutchley until 1839 or Turner until 1845. A second Australian Hudson found Mikawa at 1101. Its report, which again was sent only when the aircraft returned from its flight, was not received by Turner until about 2230.

These delays were disastrous. Had prompt warning been given, MacArthur or McCain could have dispatched other flights which might have been able to give a correct assessment of the enemy's strength. For, by a crowning misfortune, the Hudsons' reports were unreliable. The first referred to 'three cruisers, three destroyers, two seaplane tenders or gunboats', the latter to 'two heavy cruisers, two light cruisers and one unidentified vessel'.

If these descriptions had been prepared by the Japanese they could scarcely have proved more deceptive. The number of cruisers reported did not indicate sufficient fire-power for an attack on the Allied landing-forces. On the contrary the presence of two seaplane tenders suggested that the enemy planned to set up a new seaplane base. Turner was convinced that the destination of the vessels sighted was Rekata Bay on the north-west of Santa Isabel, some 150 miles from Guadalcanal, whence air attacks on his command could be renewed. He was fortified in this belief by a signal from MacArthur's headquarters at about 2000, giving a similar assessment of Japanese intentions.*

Furthermore Turner had previously requested McCain to arrange a special reconnaissance over the enemy's most likely approach route through the Slot. Bad weather had forced the scout to turn back but Turner was never informed of this. He therefore concluded that the absence of any further sightings was a confirmation that the Japanese vessels had indeed left the Slot, heading for Rekata Bay.

There was thus no sense of urgency as the Allied naval forces took up routine defensive positions for the night of 8/9th August. Weak screens of destroyers and minesweepers protected the transports off Guadalcanal and Tulagi. Rear-Admiral Norman Scott with light cruisers *San Juan* (his flagship) and HMAS *Hobart* and destroyers *Monssen* and *Buchanan* covered the eastern approaches to the beach-

* By an odd irony, on 8th August a Japanese flying-boat support ship, *Akitsushima*, really was coming down the Slot; preparing to establish a seaplane base at Gizo Island, west of Kolombangara.

Henderson Field, Guadalcanal, shortly after its capture by the Americans.

US Transport *George F Elliott* on fire, 8th August 1942.

Japanese Heavy Cruiser *Chokai*.

heads. And Crutchley with six cruisers and six destroyers moved into the channel between Guadalcanal and Florida Island to guard against an attack from the west.

The screen commander's dispositions (which were approved by Turner) were not well judged, although doubtless their deficiencies appeared more obvious later than at the time. At the entrance to the channel a small, steep, jagged volcanic cone rears abruptly from the ocean depths. This is Savo Island from which the coming battle would take its name. Crutchley would have done better to have taken all his ships to the west of this, where his cruisers could have operated together with plenty of sea room. Instead he stationed them in the confined waters east of Savo, where they had to be divided into two separate units which would be unable to support each other in the event of an attack.

Of these, the Southern Group, consisting of heavy cruisers HMAS *Australia* (flagship) and *Canberra* and USS *Chicago*, escorted by destroyers *Patterson* and *Bagley*, remained under Crutchley's own command. Its duty was to block the strait between Guadalcanal and Savo. That of guarding the passage between Savo and Florida was entrusted to Captain Frederick Riefkohl, skipper of heavy cruiser *Vincennes*, who had with him two other American heavy cruisers, *Quincy* and *Astoria*, and two destroyers, *Helm* and *Wilson*; yet since Crutchley had not prepared a battle plan, Riefkohl's Northern Group had no idea how it was expected to operate should a surface action develop.

As outlying sentinels, Crutchley had stationed destroyers to the north-east and north-west of Savo : the *Ralph Talbot* and *Blue* respectively. Both were fitted with radar, which none of the Japanese ships possessed, but since their movements were not co-ordinated, they were at times as much as twenty miles apart, which left a sizeable gap in their radar coverage. They were also positioned too near the cruisers to give the latter enough time to act on any warning received and too close to the island to allow their radar – which being of the SC type was in any case designed primarily to detect aircraft* – to function with maximum efficiency.

Crutchley's forces were neither trained nor equipped for the coming

* The only vessel equipped with the new SG surface search radar was Scott's *San Juan*.

encounter. The ships had not fired their guns at a target by night during the previous eight months. The American star-shells were ineffective; the American torpedoes notoriously unreliable. Worst of all the crews were mentally unprepared. A lack of radio discipline allowed the excellent American TBS system* to be cluttered up by unnecessary chatter, which practically guaranteed that vital messages would not be received. The lookouts, understandably tired in the steaming, exhausting heat of the Solomons, showed little alertness; those on the cruisers seem to have relied on the picket destroyers; those on *Ralph Talbot* and *Blue* to have trusted in the probing beams of their radar, the limitations of which had not yet been appreciated.

Behind all the errors lay the fundamental misapprehension that the Japanese could not fight at night. Certainly Rear-Admiral Turner was convinced of this. His great anxiety was what would happen next morning when Fletcher's retirement would leave him at the mercy of renewed air-raids. Reluctantly he concluded that he had no choice but to withdraw his transports before such attacks could be launched. At 2032 therefore, he summoned Vandegrift and Crutchley to his flagship *McCawley* to discuss the situation. The screen commander, equally confident that the enemy posed no immediate threat, set out for the rendezvous not in his barge or in a destroyer but in his flagship *Australia*, thereby depriving the Southern Group of a third of its 8-inch guns.

Crutchley directed Captain Howard Bode† of *Chicago* to take command of the Group but since Bode believed that his superior would return shortly, he did not trouble to bring his ship into station ahead of *Canberra*. Soon afterwards he retired to his bunk. No one thought to inform the luckless Captain Riefkohl that he was now the senior officer in the Savo area.

At the conference on *McCawley*, both Crutchley and Vandegrift supported Turner's decision to withdraw, the General with a reluctance that can be imagined. Crutchley went back aboard *Australia* soon after 0100 but rather than try to rejoin his Group on a pitch-black night when the stars had been blotted out by cloud, he decided to keep his flagship on patrol to the west of the Guadalcanal transports. By this time, in any event, disaster was already almost inevitable.

* The initials stood for 'Talk Between Ships'.
† Pronounced to rhyme with Cody.

The casualness of the defenders contrasted sharply with the eager anticipation of the Japanese as they prepared for 'the traditional night attack of the Imperial Navy'. Mikawa's ships were steaming in single line ahead, flagship *Chokai* in the van, followed by *Aoba*, *Kako*, *Kinugasa* and *Furutaka* in that order, then light cruisers *Tenryu* and *Yubari*, with destroyer *Yunagi* bringing up the rear. At 2313, *Chokai*, *Aoba* and *Kako* launched their seaplanes to check on the position of the Allied ships and to illuminate them with parachute flares at the right moment.*

As these scouts approached, *Ralph Talbot* sighted one, while *Blue* located another on her radar. Unfortunately their signals never reached Rear-Admiral Turner. The cruisers of the Northern Group also saw the Japanese but as these were nonchalantly showing red and green navigation lights, Captain Riefkohl assumed they must be friendly. Not long afterwards he turned in, as the other cruiser captains had already done. For the best part of two hours, the seaplanes prowled about over the Allied shipping, dimly but sufficiently visible in the light cast by the burning, derelict hulk of the *George F. Elliott*, sending back a steady flow of useful information to Vice-Admiral Mikawa.

At 0054, the first surface-sighting was made, not by American radar but by the sharp eyes of a lookout on *Chokai* who reported a destroyer on the starboard bow heading away from the Japanese column to the south-west. No one on the *Blue* – for such was the Allied vessel – spotted the big cruiser with its massive bridge containing fire control and communications equipment and with its high, white bow wave. Though all guns were trained on *Blue* in case she should react, Mikawa rightly decided not to give a warning by firing on this minor target. Instead, reducing speed to 22 knots, he turned to port, intending to pass north of Savo.

Shortly afterwards, his lookouts reported *Ralph Talbot*; her log suggests she was too far away to have been sighted but there seems little doubt that her position had not been plotted correctly. She also was steaming away – to the north-east. As *Blue* still made no challenge, Mikawa reverted to his original decision to steer south of Savo. By 0132, he had again increased speed to 26 knots, had rounded the

---

* *Kako*'s aircraft did not return but was lost together with its crew.

island and had turned on an easterly course for the final advance on his prey.

Two minutes later, yet another American destroyer came into view. This was the damaged *Jarvis*, whose skipper, Lieutenant-Commander Graham, was anxious to get to Sydney as soon as possible for the repairs that would enable his ship to return to the combat area. *Jarvis* apparently did not observe the enemy column, though it is just possible that she was unable to give the alarm because of previous damage to her communication system. Again the Japanese held their fire but Mikawa detached destroyer *Yunagi* to ensure that *Jarvis* did not interfere later. At 0136, bigger game was detected: Bode's Southern Group.

This force was moving north-west at 12 knots with *Canberra* and *Chicago* in line ahead while destroyers *Patterson* and *Bagley* screened *Canberra's* port and starboard bow respectively. At 0138, the 'Long Lances' leaped out of their tubes, aimed at *Canberra*, *Chicago* and *Bagley*. Yet it was another five minutes before an Allied ship finally noticed the Japanese. 'Warning! Warning! Strange ships entering harbour!' called destroyer *Patterson* but in the bedlam on the TBS circuit few other Allied vessels heard her.

In any case the alarm came too late. At almost the same instant, the Japanese seaplanes dropped some brilliant parachute flares, silhouetting the Southern Group for Mikawa's gunners, who had shown such restraint when tempted by destroyer targets but who now hurled a storm of shells at the bewildered Allied cruisers.

Surprise was total. On the *Canberra*, the alarm bell was clanging, the crew was rushing to action stations, but the gun-turrets were still trained fore and aft, when the tracks of torpedoes were seen on both sides of the vessel. Morison reports that two of these struck the heavy cruiser on her starboard side, a view that is echoed by Captain S. W. Roskill in the British Official History of *The War at Sea** but is denied by a subsequent RAN Board of Enquiry held at Sydney. There is no argument that she was hit by at least 24 shells – 8-inch and smaller – in about one minute. These tore open her hull, wrecked her upperworks and started fires. Below decks both boiler rooms were flooded, all light and power failed and *Canberra* was left dead in the water.

* Volume II: *The Period of Balance.*

84 of her crew died, including Captain Getting; 55 more were injured. A shell also struck little *Patterson*, knocking out two of her guns. Her casualties were eight killed, eleven wounded.

Astern of *Canberra*, USS *Chicago* swerved desperately to avoid torpedoes racing in on her starboard bow. Immediately afterwards, more of the deadly 'fish' were sighted to port. Again the wheel was put hard over but at 0147, a 'Long Lance' exploded against *Chicago*'s bow, blowing out the bottom of her cable locker. At the same moment, a shell hit high up on the foremast, sending splinters flying over the deck; they killed two and wounded 21 of her crew.

By this time the enemy had already passed ahead of the Southern Group. So swiftly had the encounter taken place that *Patterson* was unable to reach a position from which to launch her torpedoes, though she fired her remaining guns briskly if ineffectively; while *Bagley* sent her torpedoes vainly in the wakes of the Japanese warships as these were speeding away from her.

On *Chicago*, no one had realized that the hostile cruisers now lay to the north-east. Captain Bode, who had been awakened from a sound sleep, ordered star-shells to be fired. Of four salvoes – sixteen shells – not one ignited. But at this moment Bode sighted a search-light to the west. Destroyer *Yunagi*, determined to play her part in the fighting, was trying to illuminate *Jarvis* which she believed was a light cruiser. Shortly afterwards at 0152, she opened fire on *Jarvis*, on which she inflicted further damage, though not nearly as much as the Japanese believed.

Yunagi's aggressiveness, however, was well repaid. Increasing speed to 26 knots, *Chicago* headed in her direction. During the next two hours, the bewildered Bode hunted for *Yunagi* without success. Nor did he prevent the Japanese destroyer from making another attack on poor *Jarvis* at 0200. *Chicago*, like *Canberra* though for different reasons, was out of the battle.

Meanwhile at 0146, lookouts on *Tenryu* had sighted the vessels of the Northern Group whose approximate position had already been given to Mikawa by his aerial scouts. *Chokai* therefore changed course to east-north-east. *Aoba*, *Kako* and *Kinugasa* followed her but *Furutaka* apparently was taken by surprise by this manoeuvre. To avoid a collision with *Kinugasa*, she turned slightly to starboard, then back to port, heading north-by-east. *Tenryu* and *Yubari* steered in the

same direction, the three of them forming a separate column roughly
parallel to the group led by *Chokai* but about two miles to the west.
Both Japanese sections charged towards their new victims.

The three heavy cruisers of the Northern Group were steering north-
west, *Vincennes* in the lead, followed by *Quincy*, then *Astoria*, with
destroyer *Helm* to port and destroyer *Wilson* to starboard. Captain
Riefkohl had seen the flares, had heard and seen gunfire, but, believing
that the Southern Group were shooting at aircraft, he took no action
apart from increasing speed from 10 to 15 knots. His optimism has
been severely criticized by Morison among others, yet it was understandable since in the confusion Captain Bode had failed to notify
him of the presence of enemy surface vessels.

Thus Riefkohl's force also was unprepared for action when, at 0148,
Chokai fired torpedoes at the nearest American vessel, *Astoria*; fortunately they missed. Two minutes later, *Chokai*'s searchlight, stabbing
out of the darkness, fastened on *Astoria*. Seconds afterwards, *Aoba*'s
searchlight illuminated *Quincy* – so brightly that the Japanese lookouts
could see that her turrets were still trained fore and aft – while that
of *Kako* fell on *Vincennes*. Japanese gunfire followed, the tall pillars
of water from 8-inch shells towering up alongside all three targets.

Yet still most Americans could not believe that the enemy was upon
them. Riefkohl, certain that the searchlights came from the Southern
Group, demanded over the TBS that they be switched off. On
Quincy, Captain Moore ordered: 'Fire at the ships with the searchlights on!' Two salvoes promptly left *Quincy*'s guns, but Moore then
changed his mind. Fearing that a terrible mistake was being made, he
ceased fire and turned on his ship's recognition lights. *Astoria* also
opened fire by command of her Gunnery Officer, Lieutenant-
Commander Truesdell. Only one salvo had been hurled at *Chokai*,
however, when Captain Greenman, who had been asleep in his
emergency cabin, reached the bridge, shouting to Lieutenant-
Commander Topper, Officer of the Watch: 'Who sounded the general
alarm? Who gave the order to commence firing? Topper, I think we
are firing on our own ships, let's not get excited and act too hasty.
Cease firing!'

Such hesitation was fatal. As *Astoria*'s guns fell silent, three more
salvoes from *Chokai* crashed into the sea, each closer than the one
before.

'Sir,' pleaded Truesdell, 'for God's sake give the word Commence Firing!'

With the despairing remark, 'Whether our ships or not, we will have to stop them', Greenman did so. It was too late. The next salvo struck *Astoria* amidships with such force that to the watching Japanese she 'seemed to break in two'. Flames burst from her superstructure, increased by fuel pouring from a shattered seaplane on its catapult.

An almost identical series of events took place on *Quincy*. Here too, as his officers tried to persuade the captain to reverse his decision, a salvo, from *Aoba*, burst aboard her. Again one of her scouting aircraft caught fire, enveloping her in flames from midships aft – though her forward guns now re-opened fire. *Vincennes*, after firing a salvo of star-shells from her 5-inch battery to illuminate her targets, got off two salvoes from her 8-inch guns. A shell from the second of these hit *Kinugasa*, though her total casualties were only four seamen killed and another wounded. Simultaneously shells from both *Kako* and *Kinugasa* crashed into *Vincennes* amidships. Once more her aircraft on their catapults flamed like torches. Riefkohl turned first to port, then to starboard to try to escape, but the burning cruiser made an easy mark for further hits.

Five ghastly minutes had passed since the searchlights had come on. By this time the three detached Japanese vessels – which for the sake of convenience may be termed the *Furutaka* section – were also blazing away at the American cruisers. And now the 'Long Lances' arrived to strike the final blows. One for certain, perhaps two, tore open *Quincy*'s side. Two, possibly three, exploded against *Vincennes*.

Since of the American destroyers, *Wilson* exchanged only a few useless shots with *Chokai* which she had glimpsed vaguely, while *Helm* was unable to locate a single enemy vessel, the Northern Group was already finished as an effective fighting unit. Mikawa, therefore, at 0200, turned *Chokai* to starboard, hoping to lead his other ships against the transports. However in the frenzy of action they continued on their original course, sweeping round behind, then onto the starboard flank of the Northern Group, which was thus caught in a crossfire between them and the *Furutaka* section. Mikawa accordingly turned back, to take up station behind *Kinugasa*. As he did so, two shells hit *Chokai*, one doing little harm but the other destroying the Admiral's staff chartroom, killing 34 men, wounding 32.

Mikawa recalled after the war that 'the centre ship of the Northern Group' returned the heaviest fire of any American cruiser, so it seems probable that these blows were struck by *Quincy*, though it is surprising that any ship in that Group was still capable of putting up resistance of any kind. Both *Astoria's* forward turrets were knocked out. Fires burned throughout her length. *Quincy* was already down by the bow. Her No 2 turret exploded after a direct hit. Her sick bay was wiped out. A shell found her bridge, fatally wounding Captain Moore and killing almost every other person present. Another blew up the ammunition of a 5-inch gun, slaughtering all in its vicinity. *Vincennes* too had lost her forward turrets. At $0203\frac{1}{2}$, a torpedo from *Yubari* hit her port side aft, increasing her list to port. All three came to a halt, completely disabled.

Unbelievably, however, when two more searchlights found *Vincennes* it was believed that they were from friendly ships because they appeared from a new quarter – the Japanese main section had now pulled ahead of the starboard side of the American column. Riefkohl ordered a large battle ensign hoisted at the foremast. It promptly brought a renewed hail of fire from the enemy who thought it was an Admiral's flag. At about 0215, the last American shots of this stage of the action were fired by *Astoria*, one of them hitting a forward turret on *Chokai* but doing little damage. At almost the same moment the searchlights went out; the Japanese guns also fell silent.

Two minutes later, they opened up again further north. *Furutaka*, *Tenryu* and *Yubari*, sighting *Ralph Talbot*, fired seven salvoes at her, making only one hit. Lieutenant-Commander Callahan thought, as his superiors had done previously, that he was being attacked by his own side. He switched on his recognition lights and called out his identification over the TBS. Confused by this unexpected response and fearing that their target might be *Yunagi*, the Japanese ceased fire.

The respite was only temporary. Light cruiser *Yubari* turned on her searchlight, the beam of which lit up *Ralph Talbot's* bridge. More shells followed, four of which struck the American destroyer. She fired back gamely; she also sent four torpedoes at her attackers, though without result; but, ablaze, listing to starboard, with twenty-two casualties, eleven of them fatal, she was saved from destruction only by a heavy rainstorm which swept over her.

By this time Vice-Admiral Mikawa had decided that he would not prolong his visit. Though Turner's transports were at his mercy, he knew that it would be some while before he could rally his scattered vessels, he feared that daylight would bring heavy attacks from Fletcher's carriers and it may be that he felt that fortune which had hitherto favoured him so conspicuously might not continue to smile.

So by about 0240, when *Chokai* had regained her place at the head of the heavy cruiser column, Mikawa ordered speed increased to 30 knots for a hasty retreat up the Slot. The *Furutaka* section followed him, while the aggressive *Yunagi*, which had retired to the south and west of Savo, fell in astern of *Yubari*. The action was over.

Though Yamamoto signalled his appreciation of 'the courageous and hard fighting of every man in your organization', in private he rebuked Eighth Fleet's commander for not attacking the transports. There is no doubt that Mikawa's withdrawal was a crucial moment in the campaign. As Roskill remarks : 'Mikawa undoubtedly thereby sacrificed the chance of inflicting a defeat which would have brought disaster to the whole Allied expedition'; while Vice-Admiral Friedrich Ruge in *Sea Warfare 1939–1945: A German Viewpoint* states that by failing to engage the transports, 'Mikawa missed one of the greatest opportunities of the war'.

It is true that many accounts excuse Mikawa's action on the ground that he could reasonably anticipate strikes from American aircraft next morning. Bearing in mind, however, that he had already accepted that he would have to face these at some time during his retirement, it seems unarguable that he should have ignored the risks involved and annihilated the transports, particularly as they had rightly been regarded as the primary strategic objective.

Perhaps Mikawa would have done if only he had known the full extent of the chaos prevailing among his foes. When Bode brought *Chicago* back from a futile chase of *Yunagi*, he encountered *Patterson* standing by the crippled *Canberra*. A brisk though mercifully in-accurate exchange of gunfire followed before the misunderstanding was corrected by an emergency identification signal from the destroyer. Meanwhile several other destroyers, mis-reading an order from Crutchley to rally to *Australia* as a command to proceed to a rendez-vous previously arranged in case of trouble, sped away to a position five miles north-west of Savo whence they would be unable to be a threat to either friend or foe.

The screen commander was also desperately trying to assess the situation by radioing: 'Are you in action?' to his scattered vessels. 'Were but not now,' answered Bode curtly. Rear-Admiral Scott who had not taken part in the fighting could give no information of value. Ominously the Northern Group did not reply at all.

At 0235, Ironbottom Sound first earned its gruesome name as USS *Quincy* capsized to port and slid bow-first to the depths. Captain Moore, whose body was washed up on Savo Island, and 369 others died, while 167 were wounded but survived. Fifteen minutes later, *Vincennes* also rolled over and sank. Her losses totalled 332 dead, 258 injured.

Throughout the remainder of the night, the survivors, some burned, others wounded, many covered with oil, clung to life rafts, or floating crates, or even empty shell cases. Captain Riefkohl swam from one group to another, giving what aid and encouragement was possible. From time to time a sailor would vanish with ghastly suddenness; next morning, riflemen on the rescuing destroyers killed about a dozen sharks.

Dawn on 9th August revealed *Canberra* and *Astoria* still afloat – but already by 0500, Turner had commanded that the Australian cruiser either join him by 0630, to retire from the area, or be abandoned. Since *Canberra* was dead in the water, listing and burning, Commander Walsh who had succeeded the mortally wounded Captain Getting had no option but to begin the transfer of his crew to *Patterson*. The evacuation was interrupted by the clash with *Chicago* already mentioned but by 0640, 680 survivors were safely aboard either *Patterson* or *Blue* which had also come to assist.

Turner's order, not well received by *Canberra*'s men at the time, has been the subject of much debate since. As we have seen, there is a disagreement as to whether or not the cruiser had been hit by the 'Long Lances', but in any case it took over 300 shells and two torpedoes from destroyers *Selfridge* and *Ellet* to send her to the bottom at about 0800. It is difficult therefore to blame those Australians who feel that she was sacrificed unnecessarily.*

* Since *Canberra* was only the last of a series of naval losses which the Australians had suffered, Britain transferred another 8-inch cruiser to them as a replacement. This vessel, the *Shropshire*, served with distinction during the latter part of the Pacific War, notably at the Battle of Leyte Gulf.

Australian bitterness was increased by the fact that not only did Turner not retire from the area but attempts to save USS *Astoria* continued through the morning with the aid of destroyers *Bagley* and *Wilson* and minesweeper *Hopkins*. Despite all efforts, however, her fires spread. At 1100, a magazine explosion sealed her fate. Destroyer *Buchanan* and supply ship *Alchiba* took off her crew. At 1215, *Astoria* finally fell over on her port side and disappeared beneath the waves. Of her crew, 216 had died, 186 had been wounded.

With about 1,000 survivors to be rescued from the sea, with wounded needing attention and with the evacuation of *Canberra* and *Astoria* to complete, there could in practice be no question of Turner carrying out his planned early withdrawal. Instead he continued unloading supplies until about 1600, piling these up on the beaches if they could not be moved inland.

Fortunately this action did not result in further casualties. Although Rear-Admiral Yamada sent off a strike of sixteen torpedo-carrying Bettys, escorted by fifteen Zeros, their targets were not Turner's transports but Fletcher's carriers. These were already too far south to be found but at about 1300, the Japanese sighted destroyer *Jarvis* (which they mistook for a cruiser) down at the bow and trailing oil. Her crew must have known they were doomed for Lieutenant-Commander Graham had jettisoned all boats and rafts before leaving Guadalcanal in order to save weight. They put up a brief, desperate resistance, downing two Bettys, damaging four more, before their vessel, torpedoed repeatedly, was sent to the bottom with every man of her crew of 247.

In contrast, Mikawa's raiders who were expecting air attacks, were left untroubled.* They were not, however, to return to base unscathed. On the afternoon of the 9th, feeling safe from American airmen, Mikawa detached Rear-Admiral Goto with *Aoba*, *Kako*, *Kinugasa* and *Furutaka* to proceed to Kavieng, while *Chokai*, *Tenryu*, *Yubari* and *Yunagi* continued to Rabaul. Next morning, submarine *S-44* sighted Goto some 70 miles from port. Lieutenant-Commander Moore must have thought that all his prayers had been answered: the four

---

* Captain Forrest Sherman of *Wasp*, hearing a report of the fighting at about 0300, begged for permission to turn back and launch aircraft at daybreak in pursuit of the Japanese ships, but his superior officer, Rear-Admiral Noyes, refused even to forward his request to Fletcher.

heavy cruisers had no destroyer escort, while just a solitary aircraft
flew above on anti-submarine patrol.

Cautiously, Moore closed to within 700 yards of his target, undetected. At 0908 10th August, four torpedoes crashed into *Kako*.
She broke in half, to sink within five minutes. In the confusion, the
submarine slipped quietly away.

The battle provided many lessons from which the Americans later
benefited. Communications were improved. Inflammable material
was banned from all ships : wooden, heavily upholstered wardroom
furniture was removed and the layers of paint and linoleum on bulk-
heads and decks were scraped off down to the bare steel : 'day and
night for the rest of 1942,' says Morison, 'sounds of chipping hammers
were never still.' Better fire-fighting equipment was introduced, notably
the 'fog nozzle' which poured a mist of water vapour on the flames,
far superior to the solid streams from hoses. The knowledge gained at
such high price at Savo Island would save many ships and many men
in later actions.*

The Marines had no such consolations to raise their morale when,
in the late afternoon of 9th August, Turner's transports, covered by
what remained of the escorting warships, left Ironbottom Sound for
Noumea with much of their cargoes still on board, including all heavy
artillery, all landmines, all radar equipment, all camouflage netting,
all spools of barbed wire except eighteen, all heavy construction equipment except one bulldozer, most of the ammunition and about half the
supplies of food. Had the earlier air attacks hit the dumps on the
beaches, or had Mikawa smashed the transports, Operation 'Watchtower' would have collapsed entirely. As it was, Vandegrift's men, with
enough ammunition for four days' fighting and rations, which if served
in only two meals a day, could last about a month, faced a grim
future.

Of the officers whose decisions had been responsible for this
calamity, Rear-Admirals Turner and Crutchley were lucky enough to
be judged 'in no way inefficient, much less at fault' by the usually
unforgiving Admiral King. Turner at least repaid this generosity
by becoming, in Morison's words, 'a practitioner of amphibious war-

---

* Though the Royal Navy had forgotten it again by the time of the Falklands
conflict in 1982.

fare second to none', commanding successful landings on the central Solomons, Makin, Kwajalein, the Marianas, Iwo Jima and Okinawa. Vice-Admiral Fletcher also escaped formal blame though it seems that his errors were remembered against him later. Captain Riefkohl of *Vincennes* who had behaved so well after his ship had gone down, was heart-broken by her loss and that of her squadron-mates. He was not given another sea command. Captain Bode of *Chicago* shot himself.

CHAPTER THREE

The Battle of the Eastern Solomons

From the moment of Turner's retirement on 9th August, the whole struggle for Guadalcanal may be summarized in one word: 'supplies'. The Americans had gained what President Roosevelt called 'a toe-hold in the Southwest Pacific' but if they were to retain this, then more men, equipment and particularly aircraft would have to be brought in to aid the Marines. Until that time, Vandegrift's troops were in the position of a besieged garrison, threatened by air-raids, naval bombardments and counter-attacks on land.

Fortunately, only the first two threats were realized while the Americans were at their most vulnerable. From 10th August onwards, Japanese bombers regularly pounded their airfield, at first from 10,000 feet, but after the 12th, when AA fire severely damaged five Bettys, from 25,000 feet, with a consequent decline in accuracy. There were also occasional raids at night which did little harm but contributed to the strain on the defenders. Destroyers or submarines periodically patrolled off-shore out of range of the few American artillery pieces. This evidence of enemy superiority at sea probably did more damage to morale than the Japanese shells caused to shore installations.

In contrast, the Japanese ground troops, who had withdrawn across the Matanikau River to the west of the airfield, were incapable of challenging the Americans' 'toe-hold', though they quickly proved that they were not to be treated lightly. A captured Japanese naval warrant officer, after being given a couple of glasses of brandy, stated that his comrades were so short of supplies that they were eager to surrender. Recent experiences on Tulagi, Gavutu and Tanambogo cast considerable doubt on the reliability of this information but unhappily a patrol near the mouth of the Matanikau had recently reported –

quite erroneously – that a 'white flag' had been shown by an enemy detachment.*

Accordingly Lieutenant-Colonel Goettge, the Division Intelligence Officer, determined to lead a reconnaissance in the area. Vandegrift expressed doubts but the Colonel insisted, declaring : 'The way to get intelligence about the enemy is to go where the enemy is.' Shortly before midnight on 12th August, his patrol of 25 men came ashore from a landing-craft. They had hardly moved off the beach before they ran into an ambush from which only three NCOs ultimately escaped to make their way to their own lines.

This minor incident almost had major consequences. Among the Americans who lost their lives was an interpreter named Lieutenant Ralph Cory who had previously served with the Office of Naval Communications, where he had been one of those engaged in translating intercepted signals. That he had been allowed to enter a combat zone at all is incredible. Had he been taken alive, the Japanese might have discovered that their codes were being read. The knowledge would have resulted in drastic changes in their cryptographic systems which might well have deprived the Americans of their priceless knowledge of enemy plans for the whole of the rest of the war.

The depression caused by the patrol's loss was lifted on 15th August, when destroyer-transports *Colhoun*, *Gregory*, *Little* and *McKean* landed supplies and personnel for Henderson Field : a small operations detachment headed by Major Hayes, a 120-man-strong maintenance unit led by Ensign Polk, 400 drums of aviation fuel, almost 300 bombs, aircraft ammunition, tools and spare parts. On the 20th, the first three were back again, this time bearing 120 tons of rations.

Meanwhile on 12th August, an amphibious Catalina piloted by an aide of Rear-Admiral McCain had made a trial landing on the air-strip. On the 17th, Vandegrift notified Ghormley that this was ready for use. Three days later, escort carrier *Long Island*† from a position south-east of San Christobal, launched twelve Dauntless dive-

---

* It appears that this was really nothing more than an ordinary Japanese flag which by pure chance happened to have been folded in such a way that the 'sun' emblem in the middle had been concealed.

† This vessel was the first of the little American escort carriers, hastily converted from merchantmen to meet the needs of war. She had previously been the transport SS *Mormacmail*.

bombers of Major Richard Mangrum's Marine Squadron 232, followed by nineteen Wildcats of Captain John Smith's Marine Squadron 223. An hour later they reached Henderson Field to provide Vandegrift with 'one of the most beautiful sights of my life'. As Mangrum climbed out of the cockpit, the General stepped forward to wring his hand.

Next day, four of the fighters intercepted an enemy raid, Smith shooting down one of the escorting Zeros, though the Wildcat flown by Sergeant Lindley was so badly damaged that it was 'written off' in a crash landing. It was the first combat recorded by what became known – after Guadalcanal's code-name – as the 'Cactus Air Force'.

From that moment, the pilots met with every imaginable type of experience which many, alas, did not live to relate. Henderson Field provided a base from which bombing attacks could be launched, fighter defence could be given, but most important, aerial scouts could supply advance warning of enemy warships or transports moving towards the island, at least during daylight. As the strength of the 'Cactus Air Force' was built up, so these advantages would increase. If the Japanese did not act quickly, they risked grave consequences.

This was appreciated by Admiral Yamamoto who wrote to Mikawa: 'The situation at Guadalcanal is very serious, more serious than that which faced our fathers when they understood that they had to occupy Port Arthur before the arrival of the Baltic Fleet' – in Japan's war with Russia in 1904–1905. The Premier, General Tojo, however, did not treat the clearance of Guadalcanal with the same urgency. Although, soon after the initial American landings, he had entrusted the major responsibility for this task to the Japanese Army, he obstinately refused to allow its air arm to take part in operations over the southern Solomons. Furthermore, most of the troops in the area were already engaged in the advance on Port Moresby. However, Lieutenant-General Harukichi Hyakutake, younger brother of the Emperor's Grand Chamberlain, who commanded the Seventeenth Army based at Rabaul, was not particularly worried, since he believed that Vandegrift could muster only about 2,000 men. He therefore decided to commit the few soldiers available to him, while at the same time aiding those already on the island.

Thus on 15th August, Japanese transport aircraft dropped food, ammunition and medicine to the troops west of the Matanikau. Two

The sinking of US Heavy Cruiser *Quincy* at the Battle of Savo Island.

US Aircraft Carrier *Enterprise* under attack at the Battle of the Eastern Solomons.

Japanese Naval Aircraft: (*Top*) Zero Fighter. (*Centre*) 'Val' Dive-bomber. (*Bottom*) 'Kate' Torpedo-bomber.

days later, destroyer *Oite* brought them more supplies as well as a
reinforcement of some 200 men from the 5th Special Naval Landing
Force. Then on the night of 18/19th August, eleven destroyers raced
past the American perimeter to land a 'spearhead unit' of 916 men
from Colonel Kiyanao Ichiki's 28th Infantry Regiment at Taivu
Point about 22 miles to the east of the airfield – the first appearance
of the night surface raiders that were to become known as the 'Tokyo
Express' or 'Cactus Express' by the exasperated Americans.

It was also the first appearance of the Commander, Reinforcement
Force – at Guadalcanal, though not in the war. Rear-Admiral Raizo
Tanaka had first attracted attention during the Japanese conquest of
the Philippines, when he led the amphibious unit that took Davao,
Mindanao on 20th December 1941. Thereafter he had been responsible for the capture of several key positions in the Dutch East Indies,
before, on 27th February 1942, his destroyers had played a big part
in the Japanese victory at the Battle of the Java Sea. A small, slim
young man with a very solemn face, he hid behind a quiet, almost
shy manner, an unshakable stubborn courage, the more astonishing
because he was well aware of the lack of planning which lay behind
some of the missions with which he was entrusted during the Guadalcanal campaign and the perils with which they were beset in consequence. His unflinching resolve won the admiration even of his
enemies and there is no doubt that he will always be known by the
title that they bestowed on him : 'Tenacious Tanaka'.

Having landed Ichiki's troops, Tanaka's destroyers bombarded
American positions on Guadalcanal and Tulagi in the early morning
of 19th August. As they did so, three Flying Fortresses from Espiritu
Santo attacked *Hagikaze* and *Yamakaze*. Watchers ashore cheered
wildly as a bomb hit *Hagikaze* near her after turret. Smoke poured
from the destroyer which began to turn in circles and although she
soon repaired her damaged steering to retire safely from the area, the
incident warned the Japanese that daylight operations near Guadalcanal could be dangerous.

With vessels on both sides bringing in supplies, a clash between
them was almost inevitable. It came in the early hours of 21st August.
Two American transports, *Fomalhaut* and *Alhena*, had just arrived
at Guadalcanal escorted by destroyers *Blue*, *Henley* and *Helm*. Unknown to them, Japanese destroyer *Kawakaze* was also in the vicinity,

having landed reinforcements. As she slipped away, she encountered *Blue*, then on patrol in Ironbottom Sound.

Both destroyers made contact at almost the same moment, 0355, but whereas *Blue*'s radar did not reveal whether the strange vessel was friend or foe, *Kawakaze*'s lookouts not only spotted the American destroyer but correctly identified her. At 0359, as *Blue* moved cautiously towards her target, a 'Long Lance' crashed into her with a violent explosion which killed nine men, wounded 21, and blew her stern into a shapeless mass of twisted steel. She had to be scuttled two days later. *Kawakaze*, although strafed by aircraft from Henderson Field, returned to base with minor damage and one man wounded.

The Japanese had again demonstrated their superiority in night-fighting at sea. Fortunately for the morale of the Americans, however, they learned at the same time of their own superiority in actions on land, whether before or after dark.

Colonel Ichiki, commanding the Japanese forces at Taivu, was an experienced officer with a distinguished record in the fighting in China. Rear-Admiral Tanaka, no mean judge of such matters, has referred to his 'magnificent leadership and indomitable fighting spirit'. Yet on this occasion, he made the fatal mistake of underestimating his enemy. Believing firmly that the Americans were inferior man for man to the Japanese, he did not wait for the remainder of his regiment to join him, for artillery support, or for more than a week's rations for his men. After signalling 'we have succeeded in invasion' to Rabaul, he advanced on the Americans' 'jungle beach-head', confident that he could wipe it out with one blow.

On 19th August at about noon, a Japanese patrol of 34 men, moving westward with a complete lack of precautions, was ambushed near Koli Point by a Marine detachment led by Captain Charles Brush, so effectively that only three escaped. Maps taken from the bodies showed that an attack on the American positions was already planned. Strengthening the eastern flank of his perimeter along the river which the Marines called the Tenaru,* Vandegrift prepared for the onslaught.

---

* In reality the river was the Ilu, being wrongly identified on the Americans' inadequate maps. However, the Marine Corps still officially calls the action which was to follow, the Battle of the Tenaru River.

The destruction of his advance guard does not seem to have made Ichiki pause to reflect. 'No enemy at all, like marching through no-man's-land,' he radioed confidently. In the early hours of 21st August, his forces reached the river. Instead of swinging inland to attempt a flanking movement, they stormed across a sand-bar which at that time of year blocked its mouth. A deadly fire from Lieutenant-Colonel Pollock's battalion, carefully positioned and backed by artillery, shattered the attack. A second charge met with the same result.

Despite his mauling, Ichiki could still have saved the remnants of his command had he retired. Yet, presumably with the intention of saving 'face', he chose to hold his ground in a coconut plantation. Here his men were bombarded all next morning by artillery fire and bombed and strafed by the aircraft that had so recently arrived at Henderson Field. Meanwhile, a reserve Marine battalion, commanded by Lieutenant-Colonel Cresswell, crossed the river about a mile further inland and advanced to take the Japanese in the rear. Finally at about 1500, five light Stuart tanks, all that had been landed, moved over the sand-bar to complete the destruction; their tracks, according to Vandegrift, looked 'like meat grinders'.

The fighting ended at dusk. The Marines had lost 35 dead and over 50 wounded, a surprisingly large proportion of their casualties occurring after organized resistance had ended, as desperate, blood-soaked men, scorning surrender, rose up among the corpses to fire a last shot or throw a last grenade. But the Japanese had been all but annihilated. About 800 were dead; 30 more got away into the jungle only to die of their injuries; fifteen, all wounded, were taken prisoner. Only Ichiki, one other officer, Captain Tamioka, and a handful of survivors returned to Taivu, where the Colonel burnt his regimental colours and committed *seppuku*.

The victory at the 'Tenaru', small in size, was immense in its consequences. The Marines had out-thought, out-fought and out-manoeuvred the allegedly invincible Japanese. From now onwards, their confidence was unshakeable. And this placed the Japanese at a grave disadvantage for their tactics were designed mainly to destroy the morale of their enemies. They would charge forward ferociously, screaming war-cries, with the officers brandishing their beautiful but utterly obsolete swords. They would throw giant fire-crackers behind the American lines to make them think that they were surrounded.

Even the Imperial Army's famous infiltration movements were designed principally to cause confusion.

When fighting the Chinese, these 'terror tactics' had served the Japanese well – so well that they had never contemplated changing them. Yet against troops who refused to be 'rattled', they were frankly crude. After Ichiki's destruction, the Japanese could hope to regain Henderson Field only if they could muster enough men on the island to overwhelm the defenders by sheer weight of numbers.

To deliver the necessary reinforcements was the task of the Imperial Navy; to prevent this the task of the Navy of the United States. Another major battle between the rival fleets could not long be delayed.

*

It took place on 24th August: the Battle of the Eastern Solomons, second of the savage naval actions fought around Guadalcanal. As at Savo Island, the Japanese were the attackers, for Admiral Yamamoto intended not only to support a reinforcement convoy but also to destroy the American aircraft carriers. Each was a desirable objective but by attempting both at once the Japanese Commander-in-Chief increased the chances that he would be unable to achieve either.

Yamamoto's diverse aims were oddly reflected in his reluctance to concentrate his forces – to such an extent that some of them did not enter the combat zone at all. Battleship *Mutsu*, plus three escorting destroyers, remained to the north with the Japanese tankers, while the only contribution made by Vice-Admiral Mikawa's four surviving heavy cruisers was that their float-planes bombed American positions on the island after the main engagement was over.

Those vessels which did seek action, known as the Guadalcanal Supporting Forces, were under the overall tactical control of Vice-Admiral Nobutake Kondo, who had supported other landings during the campaigns in Malaya and the Philippines. Kondo's command included the two surviving fleet carriers of the Pearl Harbor operation, *Shokaku* and *Zuikaku*, the former flying the flag of Vice-Admiral Chuichi Nagumo, who had led the Japanese 'flat-tops' both at Pearl Harbor and at Midway – which latter defeat he was burning to avenge. Between them *Shokaku* and *Zuikaku* carried 53 Zeros, 41 Val dive-bombers and 36 Kate torpedo-bombers. The flagship also possessed a new radar set. With a range of only 40 miles it was inferior to those on Allied vessels but it did give Nagumo a benefit that he had not previously enjoyed.

Around the carriers prowled their destroyer screen – *Akigumo, Yugumo, Makigumo, Kazegumo, Hatsukaze* and *Akitsuki* – while ahead steamed battleships *Hiei* (flagship of Rear-Admiral Hiroaki Abe) and *Kirishima*, heavy cruisers *Suzuya, Kumano* and *Chikuma*, light cruiser *Nagara* and destroyers *Shikinami, Uranami, Maikaze, Nowake, Tanikaze* and *Yukikaze*. Well in advance of Nagumo's forces came Kondo's own flagship, heavy cruiser *Atago*, accompanied by four others, *Maya, Takao, Myoko* and *Haguro*, a light cruiser, *Yura*, seaplane carrier *Chitose* and destroyers *Natsugumo, Asagumo, Minegumo, Kuroshio, Oyashio* and *Hayashio*.

Yamamoto could not reasonably expect that this sizeable gathering of warships would escape detection but he hoped to direct American attention onto a sacrificial Diversionary Group which sailed with Nagumo's carriers but was detached from them before the battle opened. Commanded by Rear-Admiral Tadaichi Hara, this consisted of light carrier *Ryujo* escorted only by heavy cruiser *Tone* and destroyers *Amatsukaze* and *Tokitsukaze*.

Finally six submarines scouted ahead of the fleet, while three others took up station in the Coral Sea, west of the New Hebrides, where the American carriers were expected to operate.

While Kondo sought out the American warships, the Reinforcement Group moved directly towards Guadalcanal. Troopship *Kinryu Maru* carried 800 men from the 5th Special Naval Landing Force; four old patrol boats – the equivalents of the American destroyer-transports – carried 700 soldiers from Ichiki's 28th Infantry Regiment. They were protected, inevitably, by Rear-Admiral Tanaka's Destroyer Squadron 2 : his flagship light cruiser *Jintsu*; destroyers *Kagero, Mutsuki, Yayoi, Isokaze, Kawakaze, Suzukaze, Umikaze* and *Uzuki*.

A change in the main Japanese naval code had deprived the Americans of the detailed information of their foes' movements that they had enjoyed at Midway but 'traffic analysis' together with the ability to read certain minor codes – such as that used by the port director at Truk in the Caroline Islands where Kondo's vessels had originally assembled – at least gave warning that an attack was pending. So early on the morning of 23rd August, Vice-Admiral Fletcher's

Task Force 61, carriers *Saratoga, Enterprise* and *Wasp* with appropriate escorts, was cruising to the east of the Solomons ready for action.

At dawn, aircraft from *Enterprise* spotted two Japanese submarines proceeding southward on the surface at high speed; these they attacked unsuccessfully. A few hours later, one of Rear-Admiral McCain's Catalinas located Tanaka's transport group. On receipt of the pilot's report, Fletcher and Vandegrift decided independently to take action. At 1445 therefore, 31 Dauntless dive-bombers and six Avengers armed with torpedoes left the deck of *Saratoga*, though Fletcher prudently retained the carrier's fighters on board in case an enemy strike should also be forthcoming. About an hour and a half later, nine dive-bombers with an escort of twelve Wildcats took off from Henderson Field.

Regrettably neither of these missions was successful for the simple reason that at about 1300, Tanaka, who had reported to Rabaul that he had been sighted, was ordered to reverse course to the north. The Catalina which was still shadowing him, lost contact in almost constant rain, a relief aircraft crashed on take-off and no more was seen of the Japanese on that day.

At dusk therefore, after a vain search, the aircraft from Henderson Field returned to base where Vandegrift, despite his own anxiety, did his best to console the disappointed pilots. *Saratoga's* airmen followed them, landing on the strange air-strip with the aid of a primitive lighting system composed mainly of jeep headlights. During the night they came under a fortunately ineffective bombardment from destroyer *Kagero* which then departed smartly to re-join Tanaka. Next day, refuelled but leaving behind their 1000-pound bombs for use by the Marines, they flew back to their carrier, landing safely at 1100.

The Americans' failure to locate Tanaka had unfortunate results. Assured by Intelligence sources that the main Japanese fleet was still near Truk, so suspecting that no major action would occur for some days, Fletcher detached *Wasp* with her supporting vessels to rendezvous with tankers 240 miles to the south – though again, as Morison has shown, there was no urgent need for this. He thereby deprived his Task Force of one carrier, 80 aircraft, heavy cruisers *San Francisco* and *Salt Lake City*, light cruiser *San Juan* and seven destroyers.

However, at least the entire carrier fleet did not retire as had happened before Savo Island. *Saratoga* and *Enterprise* embarking 72 fighters, 74 dive-bombers and 30 torpedo-planes between them, were still available to oppose Kondo. The American vessels formed two separate groups about 10 miles apart around the precious 'flat-tops'. Fletcher's flagship, *Saratoga*, was guarded by heavy cruisers *Minneapolis*, *New Orleans* and HMAS *Australia*, light cruiser HMAS *Hobart* and destroyers *Phelps*, *Farragut*, *Worden*, *MacDonough* and *Dale*. *Enterprise*, flying the flag of Rear-Admiral Thomas Kinkaid, had the powerful protection of battleship *North Carolina* with an anti-aircraft armament of twenty 5-inch guns, four multiple 4-barrel 1.1-inch guns, forty 20-mm and twenty-six 0.5-inch machine-guns, heavy cruiser *Portland*, light cruiser *Atlanta* and destroyers *Balch*, *Maury*, *Benham*, *Ellet*, *Grayson* and *Monssen*.

It was as well that Fletcher was still on guard, for during the night Kondo's warriors had been heading south. At 0905 on 24th August, a Catalina spotted Hara's decoy force – *Ryujo*, *Tone*, *Amatsukaze* and *Tokitsukaze* – some 280 miles north-west of Task Force 61. A second scout reported the same group at 1128. About half-an-hour earlier, Lieutenant Richardson, a Wildcat pilot from *Saratoga*, had shot down a four-engined Emily flying-boat detected by radar, while two other Japanese reconnaissance aircraft were destroyed later.

Fletcher therefore was well aware that hostile forces were in the vicinity. He assumed, incorrectly as it chanced, that at least one of the enemy scouts had revealed his position before being downed. Yet, recalling his futile efforts of the previous day, he was rightly reluctant to launch his own aircraft. Finally he compromised by sending sixteen dive-bombers and seven Avengers from *Enterprise* on an armed reconnaissance at 1229.

Before these could hope to make contact, Fletcher's radar operators reported a group of aircraft 100 miles to the west, heading for Guadalcanal. These were six of *Ryujo*'s sixteen Kates, escorted apparently by at least fifteen of her 21 Zeros, which had taken off at 1300, to attack Henderson Field. They caused little damage in the face of fierce resistance from fourteen Wildcats, though it would be embarrassing to report the American claims in view of post-war analysis which has shown that the correct Japanese combat losses were three Kates and two Zeros. Four American fighters were also destroyed, one pilot escaping by parachute.

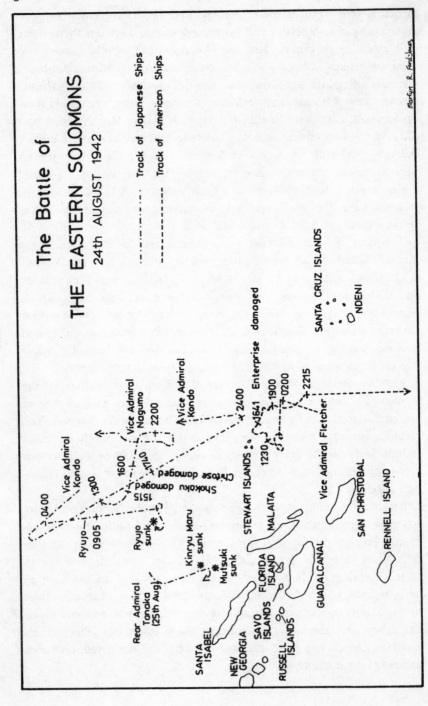

The Battle of
THE EASTERN SOLOMONS
24th AUGUST 1942

Track of Japanese Ships
Track of American Ships

Martyn R. Ford-Jones

Vice Admiral Kondo

0400

0905 Ryujo 1300

1515

Shokaku damaged

Chitose damaged

Ryujo sunk

1600

1710

2200

Vice Admiral Nagumo

Vice Admiral Kondo

2400

1641 Enterprise damaged

1230

1900

0200

2215

Vice Admiral Fletcher

Kinryu Maru sunk

Rear Admiral Tanaka (25th Aug)

Mutsuki sunk

STEWART ISLANDS

MALAITA

SANTA ISABEL

NEW GEORGIA

SAVO ISLANDS

RUSSELL ISLANDS

FLORIDA ISLAND

GUADALCANAL

SAN CHRISTOBAL

RENNELL ISLAND

SANTA CRUZ ISLANDS

NDENI

Since the radar contact confirmed earlier sighting reports of a light carrier, 30 dive-bombers and eight torpedo-carrying Avengers, led by Commander Felt, took off from *Saratoga* at 1345, to attack *Ryujo*. Fletcher would not spare them a fighter escort since he wisely retained every available Wildcat to guard his own 'flat-tops'. Nonetheless, his main striking force was now committed against a minor target, exactly as Yamamoto had planned.

Fletcher's error soon became clear as messages began to pour in from the *Enterprise* aircraft. In quick succession these sighted the *Ryujo* group, Abe's supporting vessels and, most important, Nagumo's carriers. They engaged various targets – without much success due to interceptions by enemy fighters. One Avenger was destroyed by a Zero but another Zero was accidentally brought down by Japanese AA fire.

The most gallant of these attacks came at 1515, when two Dauntlesses piloted by Lieutenant Davis and Ensign Shaw dived out of the sun on *Shokaku*, each dropping a 500-pound bomb, before escaping safely. One bomb fell just off the carrier's starboard beam; the other hit her flight deck, but unfortunately it failed to pierce this, so caused only minor damage and few casualties.

For the rest of the battle, Nagumo's big carriers suffered no further harm. Fletcher tried to divert Felt's formation onto *Shokaku* and *Zuikaku* but the usual poor radio communications thwarted all his efforts. At 1550, *Saratoga*'s airmen began their raid on the Diversionary Group.

While the major assault fell on *Ryujo*, Commander Felt directed seven dive-bombers to engage Hara's flagship, heavy cruiser *Tone*. However, after the agile little carrier had avoided the bombs dropped by every aircraft sent against her except his own, Felt ordered these seven Dauntlesses, which had just started their dives, to strike the main target instead. As they re-formed, the Commander made his own attack, his 1,000-pound bomb hitting *Ryujo* almost exactly in the centre of her flight-deck. The second wave of Dauntlesses followed him down, scoring three more hits and four very near misses. *Ryujo*'s entire hull shuddered under the explosions, while the aircraft cluttering her deck – which she had been about to launch when Felt's men arrived – burst into a 'gigantic pillar of smoke and flame', clearly visible to Tanaka, miles away over the horizon.

To complete *Ryujo*'s destruction, the Avengers, led by Lieutenant Harwood, now came in from both bows simultaneously. A torpedo tore her open below the waterline, jamming her steering gear. Burning furiously, listing twenty degrees to starboard, she turned helplessly in circles. Her escorts rescued all but 100 of her crew, before, at about 2000, she finally sank. Not one of Felt's aircraft had been lost.

Yet the Japanese considered that *Ryujo* had performed her task successfully by absorbing Fletcher's main attack. And at 1405, one of their reconnaissance aircraft had at last signalled the position of Task Force 61 to Nagumo before falling victim to the watchful Wildcats. At 1507, nine torpedo-carrying Kates, about twenty Val dive-bombers and twelve Zeros left the decks of *Shokaku* and *Zuikaku*. A few minutes later came the attack by Davis and Shaw already mentioned. It did not prevent Nagumo from sending off a second flight of nine Kates, eighteen Vals and nine Zeros at 1600. Half-an-hour later, Kondo, calling on Abe's battleship group to join him, set out aggressively to seek a surface action, his ships steaming in line abreast to increase the prospects of a sighting, while float-planes from the cruisers scouted ahead.

Meanwhile at 1602, radar gave Fletcher invaluable advance warning of the first Japanese raid, then 88 miles distant. From the decks of *Saratoga* and *Enterprise*, fifteen Wildcats soared into the air to join the 38 already on patrol over the carriers. The remaining strike aircraft on board were also launched – eleven dive-bombers and seven torpedo-planes from *Enterprise*, two dive-bombers and five torpedo-planes from *Saratoga* – with orders to counter-attack the enemy ships. Unhappily, in the confusion, they were directed not against Nagumo but against the already-doomed *Ryujo*.

The swarm of Wildcats should have been more than ample to rout the approaching raiders had they been handled correctly. Unfortunately for the fighter-director officers, however, their radar screens were cluttered with friendly aircraft on anti-submarine patrols or returning from the earlier missions, the electronic equipment installed in all American machines to send a coded signal of identity – known as IFF (Identification Friend or Foe) – failed to function adequately and worst of all, poor radio discipline led to such a bedlam of excited, unnecessary chatter between the fighter pilots that it proved impossible to issue effective instructions.

To add to the difficulties, when the Japanese sighted the *Enterprise* group at 1629, at a range of some 25 miles,* the Kate torpedo-planes descended to about 6,000 feet, while the dive-bombers, splitting into a number of small flights, climbed to about 18,000 feet. As a result, less than half the Wildcats intercepted the enemy before they reached their target and of those that did, the majority were engaged by the Zeros.

In the circumstances, the interceptors did surprisingly well. A formation from *Enterprise* broke up the attack of the Kates, destroying at least three of them. Warrant-Machinist Donald Runyon shot down three Vals plus one, possibly two, enemy fighters. The Wildcats lost five of their number to the higher-performance Zeros but they did much for future morale by inflicting heavier losses than they suffered.

Most of the dive-bombers, however, were unmolested. Taking advantage of towering cumulus clouds, they escaped detection until, at 1641, they were at last spotted as they plunged down upon *Enterprise* and battleship *North Carolina*.

At once a tremendous blast of gunfire was turned on the attackers, at least three of which blew up in mid-air while others crashed into the sea all round the vessels that they were assaulting. The small number of Vals that engaged *North Carolina* achieved only three near-misses which did no harm but though Captain Davis of *Enterprise* increased speed to 30 knots and executed a series of wild turns, the carrier could not escape. Three bombs struck her in quick succession. One burst on the flight-deck without penetrating it, but the other two, which hit almost in the same place by the after elevator, broke through to lower decks before they exploded, killing 75 men, wounding 95 more, igniting 5-inch ammunition and starting raging fires which quickly enveloped the whole area.

As the surviving raiders pulled away, every American aircraft in the vicinity turned on them. A Dauntless formation from *Saratoga*, returning from the attack on Hara, destroyed three Vals; damaged a fourth. Ensign Burnett of *Enterprise*, flying an Avenger on anti-submarine patrol, became an unofficial fighter-pilot and brought down a dive-bomber. Although American claims were greatly exaggerated –

* They at no time sighted or attacked the *Saratoga* group.

they exceeded the total of enemy aircraft present – few indeed of the Japanese returned to their carriers.

Those that did reported that *Enterprise* was doomed. She might well have been had the damage occurred earlier in the war, but past experience had caused precautions, such as draining petrol from the fuel lines, to be taken before the attack, while constant practice by damage control parties enabled the necessary action to be taken promptly after it. By 1749, the blazing 5-inch ammunition had been jettisoned, the fires were under control, though it would be some time before they were completely extinguished, and the carrier's airmen were landing back aboard her.

She was not yet out of danger, however. When the bombs had hit, fumes had begun to fill the steering-engine compartment. The men on duty had promptly shut off the ventilation system. At 1821, it was re-opened, whereupon smoke, water and fire-fighting chemicals poured into the compartment, causing an electric motor to short-circuit, thereby jamming the rudder. For 38 minutes *Enterprise* remained helpless while her crew tried desperately to rectify the situation. Finally Chief Machinist William Smith, though twice overcome by fumes, managed to start an emergency motor and the carrier's steering control was restored.

Meanwhile the second wave of Nagumo's airmen was searching for *Enterprise*. Luckily they passed about 50 miles to the westward – close enough to be detected on her radar screen – before with fuel running low, they were forced to return to their own carriers after jettisoning their weapons.

They were not the only airmen unable to find a target. Of the aircraft launched by *Enterprise* as the Japanese attack started, none made a sighting. The torpedo-planes returned to the carriers, three landing back on *Enterprise*, one of them crashing in the process, the other four going to *Saratoga*. The eleven dive-bombers, led by Lieutenant Turner Caldwell, went to Henderson Field where they provided a welcome reinforcement for the 'Cactus Air Force'. All the crews survived their experiences on the island but it was not until 27th September, that the last of them were flown out.

The aircraft from *Saratoga* were somewhat more fortunate. The five Avengers engaged Kondo's cruisers at 1735, though all their torpedoes were evaded. Two of them ditched near San Christobal, from which the crews were rescued later. The others returned to their carrier to make safe landings after dark – the first time that they had ever done this.

Meanwhile, the two Dauntlesses, flown by Lieutenant Elder and Ensign Gordon, had passed over Kondo to strike five minutes later at a target the importance of which they gleefully over-estimated. Little, thin-hulled seaplane-carrier *Chitose* bore scant resemblance to a battleship – but she had enough spirit for one and when Elder and Gordon approached, she began steaming in circles, spitting out AA fire. Unperturbed by this, the Americans attacked, scoring near-misses which flooded *Chitose*'s port engine-room; they then returned safely to *Saratoga*. Despite a list which eventually increased to thirty degrees, *Chitose* also managed to return – to her base at Truk.*

As dusk fell, Fletcher, again over-concerned about his fuel situation, retired southwards to a rendezvous with his tankers, after which *Enterprise* set out for Pearl Harbor to complete her repairs. En route, Fletcher passed the *Wasp* group coming to take up station east of the Solomons in case the fighting should be renewed next day. These vessels, however, were not to see action – a fact which in retrospect appears regrettable since Japanese aircraft losses had given the Americans a control of the skies that would have enabled them to inflict heavy punishment on their foes. Nagumo, like Fletcher, withdrew at dusk. Kondo continued to steam south but since his scouts sighted only destroyer *Grayson*, left behind to pick up the crews of aircraft which had run out of fuel, he also turned back at midnight.

Rear-Admiral Tanaka, true to his nickname, had, in contrast, no intention of retreating. During the night, five of his destroyers went ahead to bombard American positions ashore. They were attacked ineffectively by six dive-bombers, one of which was so damaged that it had to ditch. Next morning, however, at 0935, eight more dive-bombers from Henderson Field located the Reinforcement Group in daylight.

They made full use of their opportunity. Lieutenant Baldinus hit Tanaka's flagship, light cruiser *Jintsu*, between her two forward tur-

---

* *Chitose* saw further action in the Guadalcanal campaign and in January 1943, work began to convert her to a light aircraft carrier. She re-entered service in her new role a year later, taking part in the Battle of the Philippine Sea on 19th–20th June 1944, before being sunk on 25th October 1944 at the Battle of Leyte Gulf.

rets, knocking down everyone on the bridge, wrecking communications, flooding the forward magazine, starting fires and causing 61 casualties. Ensign Fink (one of the airmen Henderson Field had acquired from *Enterprise*) put a bomb into troopship *Kinryu Maru*, bringing her to a halt, burning furiously, in a sinking condition.

Hastily transferring his flag to destroyer *Kagero*, Tanaka ordered *Jintsu* back to Truk, escorted by destroyer *Suzukaze*, while another destroyer, *Mutsuki*, went alongside the doomed transport to take off her passengers and crew. As she was doing so, at 1015, eight Flying Fortresses from Espiritu Santo appeared. Anti-aircraft fire opened up but no one seemed alarmed: the Japanese were confident that high-level bombing rarely did much harm. But this time they were wrong. A near-miss damaged destroyer *Uzuki* and three direct hits crashed onto the luckless *Mutsuki* which vanished in a cloud of steam and smoke. Destroyer *Yayoi* moved in to pick up survivors, among them *Mutsuki*'s skipper, Commander Hatano, who when questioned about his experience later, remarked wryly that even B-17s hit their targets once in a while! Soon afterwards, Tanaka received orders to retire to an advance base at Shortland Island, whence the night runs of the 'Tokyo Express' would be resumed.

So ended the Battle of the Eastern Solomons. The Americans usually claim it as a victory. Certainly they had prevented the Japanese from carrying out their planned reinforcement. In addition, at a cost of seventeen aircraft from all causes, they had inflicted serious losses on Japan's naval air force which it could ill-afford. On the other hand, in return for the destruction of little *Ryujo* – which he had anticipated in his plans – Yamamoto had deprived his foes of the use of *Enterprise* for two crucial months. In view of the vital importance to the Americans of the air support provided by their carriers, it seems fair to assess the result of the action as a draw.

Furthermore the benefits gained by the Japanese from the crippling of *Enterprise* were redoubled by the other successes that they achieved in the next three weeks.

*

During those three weeks, indeed in general throughout the rest of the campaign, an extraordinary tactical situation prevailed: command of the sea changed hands every twelve hours. As Morison has vividly described the position in *The Two Ocean War* :

> The Americans ruled the waves from sunup to sundown. Big ships discharged cargoes, little ships dashed through the Sound, landing craft ran errands between Lunga Point and Tulagi. But as the tropical twilight performed a quick fadeout and the pall of night fell on Ironbottom Sound, big ships cleared out like frightened children running home from a graveyard and small craft holed up in Tulagi Harbor. Then the Japanese took over. The 'Tokyo Express' of troop-laden destroyers and light cruisers dashed in to discharge soldiers or freight where their troops controlled the beach, and, departing, tossed shells in the Marines' direction. But the Rising Sun flag never stayed to greet its namesake; by dawn the Japanese were well away and the Stars and Stripes reappeared. Such was the pattern cut to fit the requirements of this strange campaign.

American dominance of the daylight hours arose from American control of the air, which is why the crippling of *Enterprise* was such a set-back for them. If, however, Henderson Field could be developed sufficiently, the Americans would have what Rear-Admiral Turner called 'an unsinkable aircraft carrier' to provide such dominance permanently.

Many of the early American efforts, therefore, concentrated on building-up their air-strength. On 22nd August, fourteen P-400s, a development of the P-39 Airacobra, had reached Guadalcanal. Unfortunately they proved so useless in high-altitude combats with the Zeros that Vandegrift had to order that they be employed in the close-support role, for which their 37-mm cannon, six machine-guns and ability to carry a 500-pound bomb, were much better suited.

On 29th August, transport *William Ward Burrows* arrived with equipment and ground personnel for the two Marine squadrons. At 1630, she retired to Tulagi for 'greater security' – only to run aground. A good deal of her unloaded supplies had to be jettisoned during efforts to re-float her, though the rest was carried safely to Guadalcanal by a variety of small craft next day.

That same day, Colonel William Wallace led nineteen more Wildcats and twelve Dauntlesses to Henderson Field, arriving during a heavy air-raid which at least gave fair warning of what the future would hold. On 1st September, transport *Betelgeuse* brought in five officers and 387 men of a Naval Construction Battalion – Seabees as they were known – along with their equipment, which included two bulldozers; they took over the maintenance and improvement of the airfield. Two days later, Brigadier-General of Marine Aviation Roy Geiger reached the island with his Chief of Staff Colonel Woods and his Intelligence Officer Lieutenant-Colonel Munn; he assumed command of First Marine Aircraft Wing as the 'Cactus Air Force' was officially called. And on 9th September, a new fighter strip, unkindly labelled the 'cow pasture', was brought into use.

Geiger's men were inadequately supplied with fuel, ammunition, bombs, oxygen, lubricating oil and spares of every sort from tires to propellers. The airfield, constantly deluged by tropical storms, was covered alternately by a layer of black dust and a layer of black mud, over which even jeeps could only move with difficulty. In such primitive conditions, it was highly hazardous to attempt even to take-off, let alone land; on 8th September, for instance, six Wildcats were 'written off' in accidents while two others suffered severe damage.

Yet the 'Cactus Air Force' still managed to take a growing toll of the persistent Japanese raiders. On 30th August for example, eight Wildcats and eleven P-400s met eighteen Hamps* from Buka airfield, losing four of the P-400s, though two pilots baled out, but destroying seven enemy aircraft and damaging three more so badly that they did not return to base – an impressive enough achievement if less so than the destruction of all eighteen raiders as claimed by the pilots at the time.

While the Americans increased their air power, the Japanese strengthened their land forces. Hyakutake believed that 3,500 more troops under Major-General Kiyotake Kawaguchi would suffice to recapture Guadalcanal and Tanaka planned that his destroyers would take them there by night in a series of missions which were known as *nezumi* operations – the word means 'rat' in English but sounds better

---

* The Hamp was a clipped-wing variant of the Zero. Its original code-name was 'Hap' but this was altered, officially because it sounded too like 'Jap' but perhaps really because 'Hap' was the nick-name of General Henry Harley Arnold, head of the Army Air Force, who, it seems, was not amused.

Wildcat Fighters.

American Naval Aircraft.

Dauntless Dive-Bomber.

in Japanese, possibly because in that country the animal is more respected for its ability to survive by outwitting its foes in the most adverse circumstances. Tanaka certainly had many problems to circumvent, not least the interference of his superiors, for when three of his destroyers were well on their way to a planned landing on the night of 27th August, they were recalled by Vice-Admiral Mikawa.

If this decision greatly displeased Tanaka, he was to be enraged by the fate of the next reinforcement mission. Orders from Rabaul resulted in destroyers *Asagiri*, *Amagiri*, *Yugiri* and *Shirakumo* coming within range of aircraft from Henderson Field before dark on the evening of 28th August. In consequence they were first spotted by two Dauntless scouts, then at about 1800, attacked by eleven Dauntless dive-bombers. The ex-*Enterprise* pilots again did well. Ensign Fink hit *Asagiri* amidships with a 500-pound bomb, causing her to explode and sink, taking down with her the division commander, Captain Yuzo Arita. Lieutenant Caldwell hit *Shirakumo*, leaving her dead in the water. *Yugiri* suffered 'moderate damage'. Only *Amagiri* remained untouched; furthermore she shot down a Dauntless, the crew of which were killed. No troops were landed that night and the surviving destroyers, with *Amagiri* towing crippled *Shirakumo*, returned sadly to Shortland Island.

To Tanaka, this mishap 'made it more obvious than ever what sheer recklessness it was to attempt a landing operation against strong resistance without preliminary neutralization of air-power'. He was not the man to be discouraged, however. Next night, five destroyers disembarked troops at Taivu Point, while the night following, more came ashore at the same spot from destroyer *Yudachi*.

Her mission was protected by an air-strike of eighteen Bettys which, at 1512, appeared over a small American naval force off Guadalcanal: auxiliary ship *Kopara*, that had recently landed supplies, and her escorts, destroyer-transports *Colhoun* and *Little*. Choosing *Colhoun* as their target, the Japanese attacked with lethal efficiency. A series of near-misses tore their victim's sides open; brought down her foremast; twisted her 4-inch guns from their mountings; wrenched her main engines from their fastenings. Direct hits in the after deckhouse and after engine-room completed the destruction. Within two minutes of the start of the raid, *Colhoun* had disappeared beneath the waves, taking 51 of her crew with her.

Perhaps encouraged by this, eight Japanese destroyers raced through to Taivu on 31st August, to set ashore Kawaguchi and some 1,500 of his men. They held their fire when American aircraft appeared so as not to provide targets but as they made for home past Henderson Field, they shelled the Marines' positions, as much with the intention of reducing morale as in expectation of doing material damage. These 'hit and run' raids became as important a part of the duties of the 'Tokyo Express' as the landing of reinforcements. On the night of 11/12th September for instance, light cruiser *Tenryu* and three destroyers delivered a two-hour bombardment, narrowly missing Vandegrift's command post – where he was entertaining Rear-Admiral Turner who had flown in that afternoon to discuss the situation – but killing three pilots, including Lieutenant Baldinus, the man who had bombed Tanaka's *Jintsu*, and wounding two others.

Nor were Tanaka's warriors reluctant to attack any American naval vessels they encountered. In the early hours of 5th September, while another 'Tokyo Express' made a successful run to Taivu, destroyers *Yudachi*, *Hatsuyuki* and *Murakumo* had just commenced a diversionary bombardment, when, at 0100, their gun flashes were sighted by destroyer-transports *Little* and *Gregory* which were then on patrol off Lunga Point.

Commander Hugh Hadley, division commander in *Little*, at first believed the firing came from a surfaced submarine. He realized his error when radar located the enemy destroyers but before he could take further action, a Navy Catalina, flying over the area, dropped a string of flares to illuminate the intruders. Unfortunately, they illuminated *Little* and *Gregory* – of whose presence the pilot was unaware – as well. Alert Japanese lookouts quickly spotted them and the 5-inch guns swung round towards these new inviting targets.

Hopelessly outclassed, the Americans fought back despairingly but vainly. A salvo crashed into *Little*; one shell knocking out her after 4-inch gun; another jamming her rudder; a third hitting her after fuel tanks which burst into flames. Further hits followed in quick succession. Immediately afterwards, *Gregory* was also struck, her after stack knocked down, a boiler burst and fires started. Both vessels sank; *Little* with a loss of 22 killed including Hadley and her skipper Lieutenant-Commander Lofberg and 44 injured; *Gregory* with a casualty list of Lieutenant-Commander Bauer together with ten others dead, 26 wounded.

If this action confirmed the Japanese command of the sea during the hours of darkness, dawn brought with it a reminder of American domination by day. Kawaguchi had decided to land his remaining 1,000 men on the western flank of the American perimeter, but for some strange reason, preferred to transport them in barges rather than destroyers. After much argument and mainly for the sake of inter-service harmony, Tanaka had reluctantly agreed. Early on the morning of 5th September, the barges were sighted. Fighters from Henderson Field strafed them repeatedly, killing some 400 troops for the loss of one Wildcat to AA fire. However, some 300 soldiers under Colonel Oka landed safely near Cape Esperance, while 300 more found a temporary refuge on Savo, before slipping over to Guadalcanal the following night.

Indeed such was the American strength in the air that for attacks on enemy vessels by day Yamamoto had to rely mainly on his submarines. Two of these, *I-9* and *I-17*, were damaged on 25th August. *I-123* was sunk by minesweeper *Gamble* on the 28th. It was not long, however, before the United States Navy suffered far more grievous losses.

After the Battle of the Eastern Solomons, Vice-Admiral Fletcher remained in the area between San Christobal and the Santa Cruz Islands with *Saratoga* and *Wasp*, in order to protect the supply routes to Guadalcanal. On 30th August, carrier *Hornet* joined him, thereby enabling the *Wasp* group to retire to Noumea for rest and maintenance. Patrolling in a restricted area, about 170 miles long by 70 miles wide, which simplified the task of detection, and committed as they were to long periods on a steady course and speed while aircraft were landed or flown off, the 'flat-tops' could not help but be particularly vulnerable to submarine attack.

The first such came at 0748 on 31st August, when Commander Yokota's *I-26* fired six torpedoes at *Saratoga* which was then zig-zagging at only 13 knots so as to conserve her escorts' fuel. At this same moment, destroyer *MacDonough* detected the submarine and gave the alarm. Captain Ramsay rang for full speed and turned *Saratoga* hard to starboard but it was far too late. Only one torpedo found its mark; no one was killed; just twelve men, including Fletcher, were wounded; the carrier's aircraft were able to fly off safely, first to *Hornet*, later to Espiritu Santo;* yet progressive flooding caused such damage to *Saratoga*'s electric propulsion units that she had to retire to Pearl Harbor, where she remained undergoing repairs for six weeks. Fletcher, who bore the blame for this mishap, was transferred shortly afterwards to less arduous duties in the north Pacific. Despite heavy depth-charge attacks, *I-26* escaped.

The remaining American forces now moved to a new patrol area further south but six days later, torpedoes from *I-11* narrowly missed *Hornet* and *North Carolina*. The carrier, the battleship and their screening warships hastily cleared the area, then headed north of Espiritu Santo, where on 11th September, they rendezvoused with *Wasp* which had left Noumea three days earlier. On the 13th, twenty Wildcats left *Wasp*'s deck to reinforce 'Cactus Air Force', after which the combined groups took up station to provide long-range cover for a troop convoy making for Guadalcanal.

At noon on 14th September, a scouting Catalina sighted, to the north of the Santa Cruz Islands, a formidable enemy fleet which included not only *Shokaku* and *Zuikaku* but two other carriers, *Hiyo* and *Junyo*, as well. *Wasp* and *Hornet* immediately turned to the north-west and increased speed. At 1430, *Wasp* sent out scouts which were quickly followed by both dive-bombers and torpedo-planes from *Hornet*. All their efforts were wasted, however, for the enemy vessels retired to Truk soon after the strike had been launched.

The American carriers thereupon resumed their station covering the troop-transports. At 1444 on the 15th, they were some 120 miles south of the position where *Saratoga* had been hit. During the past three-and-a-half days, they had again operated in a limited area, crossing and re-crossing their old track no fewer than twelve times. They had been steaming at a speed of only 16 knots to save fuel, yet *Wasp* had slowed still more and was steering directly into the wind to launch and recover aircraft – an easy target for Commander Narahara's *I-19*. A salvo of six torpedoes leapt from the submarine's tubes.

Although Captain Sherman made a desperate attempt to escape, *Wasp* had no real chance. Three of the deadly 'fish' struck her star-

---

* All *Saratoga*'s aircraft – fighters, dive-bombers and torpedo-planes alike – were later sent by Vice-Admiral Ghormley to reinforce Henderson Field.

board side, hurling aircraft into the air, starting a heavy list, causing major fires to break out and wrecking all forward water mains, thus preventing the damage control parties from even partly checking the flames.

Some five miles north-north-east of *Wasp*, steamed *Hornet*, *North Carolina* and their escorts. They now found torpedoes racing at them. Japanese torpedoes had an amazing range and although Morison reports that another enemy submarine, *I-15*, which was in the vicinity, had fired these, it appears that in fact they were *I-19*'s remaining three. One of them had already near-missed destroyer *Lansdowne* of *Wasp*'s group. It or another now near-missed destroyer *Mustin* on *Hornet*'s port bow, before striking *North Carolina* on the port side, killing five men and tearing a hole 32 feet long by 18 feet high. The battleship stayed in formation but withdrew that evening – ultimately to Pearl Harbor for repairs.

The last two torpedoes of this extraordinary salvo threatened destroyer *O'Brien*. She managed to dodge one but the second hit her near the bow. She also retired, first to Noumea for temporary repairs, then to the United States – but her damage was more serious than had been supposed. On 19th October off Samoa, she began to break up, split in two and sank.

Wasp's end was quicker but far more horrible. Roaring flames spread throughout her length with terrifying rapidity as bombs and aviation fuel exploded, while vast columns of smoke towered overhead. At about 1500, a colossal detonation shook the carrier from end to end. Shortly afterwards, another blew the No 2 flight-deck elevator into the air. At 1520, Sherman ordered Abandon Ship, though *Wasp* lingered on, a blazing hulk, until 2100, before being finished off by three torpedoes from *Lansdowne*. Of her aircraft, 25 were airborne at the time she was hit; all except one landed safely on *Hornet*. Of her crew, 193 died; 366 were wounded.

Despite this spectacular achievement, it seems certain that Japanese submarines were far too eager to concentrate their attention on warships while, unlike their American counterparts, they tended to ignore transports as unworthy of their notice. Far more 'I-boats' should have been sent into the crucial disputed waters around the Solomons with orders to attack the American convoys. That they were not appears in retrospect to have been a fundamental mistake on the part of the

Imperial Navy, though whether such reflections consoled American seamen at the time is a different matter.

No amount of misfortune, however, could dampen the Americans' wry sense of humour. They re-christened the waters to the east of San Christobal 'Torpedo Junction'.

CHAPTER FOUR

The Battle of Cape Esperance

While *Wasp*'s crew were still struggling vainly to save her, Major-General Kawaguchi was leading the shattered remnants of his force on a long, agonizing march to safety, after his attempt to capture Henderson Field had met with a repulse as decisive and almost as complete as that suffered by the late Colonel Ichiki.

Kawaguchi had set out from Taivu with high hopes on 6th September. He had planned to launch his main attack south of the airfield on the night of the 12/13th, supported by secondary assaults across the Ilu (which the defenders still persisted in calling the Tenaru) in the east and across the Matanikau in the west. This elaborate scheme, however, took no account of the appalling country in which it had to be executed. The jungle alone was quite enough to delay the separate Japanese units; it rendered co-operation between them impossible.

Although native scouts and aerial reconnaissance had reported Kawaguchi's presence, they had greatly underestimated his strength. As a result, Vandegrift decided he would make an attack of his own on Taivu with the 1st Raider and 1st Parachute Battalions which had just been transferred from Tulagi.

At dawn on 8th September, the Americans landed from destroyer-transports *Manley* and *McKean*, *YP-289* and *YP-346*.* By a useful coincidence transports *Fuller* and *Bellatrix* also happened to appear at the same time with a destroyer escort. Thinking that a major landing was going to take place, the horrified Japanese at Taivu, who numbered only some 300 communications personnel, hastily retreated inland. The Americans advanced westward to Tasimboko

---

* YPs – 'Yippies' to the Marines – were small district patrol vessels, varying in size from 50 to 175 tons, which were used for a variety of minor tasks.

village, where, after a fierce fight, they captured a main supply depot, packed with weapons, equipment, food and medical supplies, all of which they destroyed. They then re-embarked at about 1600. Japanese reaction was prompt but hardly successful. That night, light cruiser *Sendai* and eight destroyers bombarded Tulagi, causing minor damage, while on 13th September, 26 Bettys, escorted by twelve Zeros, attacked Taivu under the mistaken impression it was still held by the Americans; they caused very heavy casualties but among their own troops.

The booty secured at Tasimboko included documents which revealed details of Kawaguchi's planned attacks. Vandegrift accordingly made preparations to meet these. He entrusted the defence in the south of the American perimeter, where he knew that the enemy's principal effort would be made, to the combined Raider and Parachute Battalion, the personnel of which, despite the Taivu raid, were less exhausted than those in any of his other units.

Examining the ground, the battalion commander Lieutenant-Colonel Edson and his second-in-command Lieutenant-Colonel Griffith* decided that its key feature was a grassy ridge, flanked by dense jungle, which ran southward for about a thousand yards from a point a mile south of Henderson Field. They moved their men there on 10th September, while Colonel del Valle, who commanded the Marine Division's artillery, brought up a number of 105-mm howitzers in close support. The position chosen had no name at the time but was soon to be given several: Edson's Ridge; Raiders' Ridge; Bloody Ridge. It began to earn the last name next morning when enemy bombers inflicted some casualties on the troops occupying it. At least this unpleasantness – which was repeated at noon on the 12th – reassured Edson that he was in the right place to thwart Kawaguchi.

That officer meanwhile was, in Griffith's words, 'clawing his way through humid, putrid jungle. Alternately soaked to the skin by torrential rains and bathed for hours in sweat, his soldiers, in a twisting column over three miles long, slipped and stumbled through ankle-deep mire as they moved foot by foot toward the positions from which they were to launch the planned surprise attack on the airfield'.

It was understandable therefore that by the time Kawaguchi reached the Ridge, his forces were already scattered. Instead of pausing to re-organize, however, he persisted in making a series of attacks on the

* Later the author of *The Battle for Guadalcanal*.

evening of 12/13th September, but these were so badly co-ordinated that the Americans defeated them without much difficulty. In the morning, Edson, who had decided that some of his forward positions were too exposed, fell back about 100 yards to an area which gave him a better field of fire and there awaited his enemy's next move.

It came on the following night. While seven destroyers bombarded Henderson Field, Kawaguchi delivered three major attacks against the Ridge. Edson's troops, brilliantly supported by the artillery which fired a total of nearly 2,000 rounds, broke all of them. Nonetheless at about 0230 on the 14th, the defenders withdrew to reserve positions, from which, with the aid of reinforcements, they threw back two further rather half-hearted assaults. A few determined Japanese, managing to slip past Edson, attacked Vandegrift's command post, a quarter of a mile away, only to be killed by his headquarters staff. As dawn broke, bringing strafing attacks from US fighters, Kawaguchi ordered a general retreat. The Americans had lost 59 killed, 204 wounded. Nearly 600 Japanese lay dead on or around the Ridge.

The secondary Japanese attacks were equally unsuccessful. The troops who struck across the upper Ilu were so exhausted from their gruelling passage through the jungle that they killed only four Americans and wounded three others before retiring with heavy losses which brought Kawaguchi's total casualties to 708 dead, 505 injured. The assault over the Matanikau did not take place until the afternoon of the 14th; it was easily repulsed.

Kawaguchi's ordeal was not yet ended. He decided not to fall back on Taivu but to join the forces under Colonal Oka to the west of the Matanikau. His men struggled through vile terrain, carrying their wounded on improvised litters. Food ran short. All weapons except rifles were abandoned. It was eight days before the half-starved survivors reached the coast, so enfeebled that for the time being at least, they were quite incapable of further action.

American morale was raised higher yet on 18th September. At 0550, Rear-Admiral Turner brought six transports with their escorting warships (which included heavy cruiser *Minneapolis*, light cruiser *Boise* and a New Zealand light cruiser *Leander*) into Ironbottom Sound.* From them were unloaded over 3,000 men of the 7th

---

* It was while giving long-range support to this convoy that *Wasp* had been lost.

Marine Regiment, tanks, vehicles, weapons, ammunition, 1,000 tons of rations and 400 drums of aviation fuel. Two of Turner's destroyers, *Monssen* and *MacDonough*, seized the opportunity to shell enemy positions, starting fires. Having embarked those members of the 1st Parachute Battalion who had survived the combat on 'Bloody Ridge', the transports retired again at dusk. In the eyes of the Marines, says Griffith, 'theUnited States Navy finally stood vindicated'.

Vandegrift now had over 19,000 men ashore and during the next couple of weeks a steady stream of Dauntlesses and Avengers arrived to increase the strength of 'Cactus Air Force'. On 30th September, Admiral Chester Nimitz flew to Guadalcanal in a Flying Fortress. Before he left next morning, Nimitz promised Vandegrift 'support to the maximum of our resources'.

Thus reinforced and encouraged, Vandegrift determined to take the initiative. Since he rightly considered that the few remaining Japanese troops to the east were no longer a threat, he directed his offensive against those on the west bank of the Matanikau. On 22nd September, his airmen made preliminary attacks, in one of which Brigadier-General Geiger personally flew a Dauntless on a bomber mission, regardless of the fact that at the age of 57 he was officially twelve years too old for such an exploit.

Next day, the Americans began a series of operations which, like those of the Japanese before them, were badly planned, because they depended on co-operation between several separate units which could not possibly be achieved in the harsh conditions of Guadalcanal. Heavy casualties were suffered in consequence. On 27th September, the dead included Major Kenneth Bailey who had won a Congressional Medal of Honor (the American VC) at the time of the defeat of Kawaguchi, when, according to Griffith, he had been 'a one-man supply section' who had made 'repeated trips on hands and knees along the fire-swept ridge to deliver grenades and ammunition'. Also on the 27th, Griffith notes that the officer commanding the 1st Raider Battalion was wounded. He modestly omits to mention that he was the officer in question.

The same day also saw the bloody defeat of a Marine landing behind the enemy lines. Its commander, Major Rogers, was killed as were 23 of his men, while a further 23 were wounded. Sergeant Robert Raysbrook, who stood up under enemy fire to signal the situation to nearby naval vessels, won a Congressional Medal of Honor. Signalman Douglas Munro of the Coast Guard, the coxswain of the leading landing craft that retrieved the survivors, who was killed while covering their withdrawal with machine-gun fire, received the same award posthumously.

Later attacks were better planned. On 9th October for instance, the Marines, aided by artillery fire, slaughtered 690 enemy soldiers whom they surprised in a bivouac area, their own casualties being 65 killed and 125 wounded – after which the Japanese withdrew their front lines about two miles west of the Matanikau.

Such successes, however, had no lasting effect; indeed while Vandegrift embarked on his limited offensive, his foes were preparing for a major one. On 31st August, Imperial General Headquarters issued instructions that the prime objective of the Japanese Army should be 'the immediate recapture of Guadalcanal', giving only a secondary priority to the campaign in New Guinea. On 18th September, the decision was taken to concentrate all possible forces against Guadalcanal. The troops in New Guinea, who had come within 30 miles of Port Moresby, were ordered to fall back to their advance base at Kokoda, there to go onto the defensive until Guadalcanal had been secured.

Lieutenant-General Hyakutake had every intention of achieving this aim without delay. He had decided to send Lieutenant-General Masao Maruyama's Second Division* to the island but since recent events had not inspired him with much confidence in his subordinates, he proposed to take personal charge of the campaign, while his Chief of Staff, Major-General Miyazaki, remained in Rabaul to co-ordinate the shipment of supplies. Yamamoto promised naval support and since it was thought that the 'Tokyo Expresses' carrying Hyakutake's troops to Guadalcanal would be subjected to air attacks, 80 bombers and 100 fighters arrived on 25th September, to reinforce the Japanese Eleventh Air Fleet in New Britain.†

* Known as the 'Sendai' Division because its men came from that northern Japanese city or its neighbourhood.

† Though it was the American dive-bombers that were most feared by the Imperial Navy, it is fair to mention that even the despised Flying Fortresses had recently scored a few hits: on heavy cruiser *Myoko* on 14th September, causing minor damage, and on light cruiser *Yura* on the 25th, putting an after turret out of action.

With their strength thus increased, the enemy airmen resumed their attempts to eliminate 'Cactus Air Force'. On 27th September, they destroyed or badly damaged five Dauntlesses and five Avengers on the airfield, but next day they were intercepted by Wildcats which, without loss, shot down four Bettys and a Zero and damaged three more Bettys so severely that they were forced to ditch on the way back to base. On 2nd October, a force of 27 Zeros caught a Wildcat formation by surprise, downing six of them and killing four of the pilots. The Americans triumphed in their turn on the following day. Nine Zeros fell to fighters or AA fire. One Wildcat was shot down though the pilot escaped by parachute; another crash-landed.

Also on 3rd October, seaplane-carrier *Nisshin* and six destroyers brought the first group of Hyakutake's soldiers to Guadalcanal. At 1725, they were attacked by seven Dauntlesses and three Avengers armed with bombs but their violent manoeuvres and heavy AA fire enabled them to escape unharmed. Another strike by five dive-bombers after dark was equally unsuccessful. During the night, the men and their equipment were landed safely and the ships retired, surviving two more air-attacks on their return journey next day.

On the 5th, nine Dauntlesses bombed a 'Tokyo Express' made up of six more destroyers. *Minegumo*, damaged by two near-misses, and *Murasame*, damaged by three, were forced to turn back. The remaining vessels were unhurt by this and a later dive-bombing attack and unloaded their reinforcements at about midnight.

Three days later, *Nisshin* and her six destroyers again broke through a series of air-raids to land men and supplies; though the Americans received some reinforcements of their own when twenty Wildcats of Marine Squadron 121, led by Major Leonard Davis and a future 'ace' (and also incidentally future Governor of South Dakota) Captain Joseph Foss, flew to Henderson Field from escort carrier *Copahee*. And at about 2230 on the 9th, light cruiser *Tatsuta* and five destroyers also defied American bombs to carry Hyakutake, his staff and a strong body of troops to Tassafaronga Point some ten miles west of the airstrip.

A bigger mission was planned for the night of 11/12th October. Rear-Admiral Takaji Joshima was ordered to sail to Tassafaronga with two seaplane-carriers, persistent *Nisshin* and newly-repaired *Chitose*, and six destroyers: *Akitsuki, Asagumo, Natsugumo, Yama-*

gumo, *Murakumo* and *Shirayuki*. On board these vessels were another swarm of soldiers and a vast amount of ammunition and equipment, including heavy field-artillery pieces that the Marines were to call 'Pistol Petes'. The responsibility for protecting this convoy – and thereafter bombarding Henderson Field – was given to Rear-Admiral Aritomo Goto, who commanded heavy cruisers *Aoba* (flagship), *Furutaka* and *Kinugasa* and destroyers *Hatsuyuki* and *Fubuki*.

On the afternoon of the 11th, a raid on Henderson Field was beaten off before it could inflict any damage but the American airmen were kept occupied to such an extent that they failed to discover the advancing Japanese naval forces. Fortunately Goto's cruisers were sighted by Flying Fortresses which tracked them as they raced south through the Slot at high speed.

It so happened that two days earlier, Rear-Admiral Turner had set out for Guadalcanal from New Caledonia with transports *McCawley* and *Zeilin*, which carried nearly 3,000 men of the 164th Infantry Regiment. Three destroyers and three minesweepers formed the close escort, while a striking force under Rear-Admiral Norman Scott provided additional protection by taking the offensive with instructions to 'search for and destroy enemy ships and landing craft'.

Scott's group, which went by the title of Task Force 64, had passed the previous three weeks in intensive training for combat by night. Its leader, an aggressive officer with a fine record, was confident that his men were now able to defeat the enemy even after dark when the Japanese had previously been considered supreme. When he received the sighting reports from the B-17s at about 1600 on the 11th, he increased speed to 29 knots and steered to intercept. Unlike Crutchley, he wisely took his ships into the open waters west of Savo Island and north of Cape Esperance, the north-west point of Guadalcanal.

Scott believed that the disaster at Savo Island had resulted largely from Crutchley's failure to concentrate the Allied forces. He therefore determined to keep Task Force 64 under his tight personal control. Accordingly, his vessels took up station in a single, continuous line ahead, about 2½ miles long. In the lead steamed destroyer *Farenholt*, on board which was the squadron commander, Captain Robert Tobin. She was followed by destroyers *Duncan* and *Laffey*; then Scott's flagship, heavy cruiser *San Francisco*. Behind Scott came light cruiser *Boise*, heavy cruiser *Salt Lake City* and light cruiser *Helena*, with

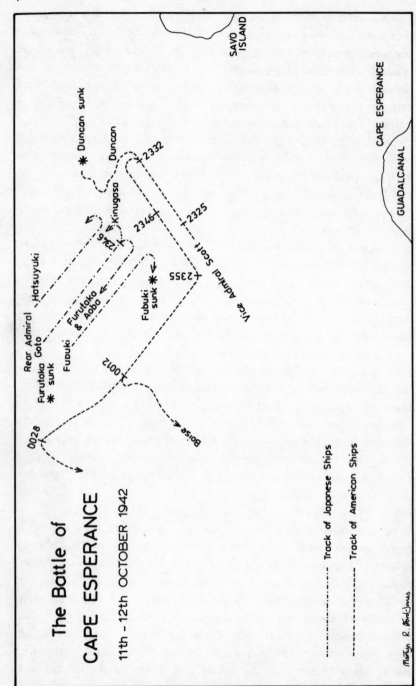

The Battle of
CAPE ESPERANCE
11th – 12th OCTOBER 1942

SAVO ISLAND

CAPE ESPERANCE

GUADALCANAL

Duncan sunk

Duncan

2332

Kinugasa

2346

2325

2346

Rear Admiral Hatsuyuki

Furutaka & Aoba

Vice Admiral Scott

Furutaka sunk

Fubuki

Fubuki sunk

2355

0012

0028

Boise

Rear Admiral
Goto

.... Track of Japanese Ships

———— Track of American Ships

Martyn R. Bond-Jones

destroyers *Buchanan* and *McCalla* in the rear. This formation was in fact dangerously unwieldy, the destroyers in particular being badly restricted by having to co-ordinate their actions with those of the much less manoeuvrable heavy cruisers.

As at Savo Island but to an even greater extent, the Americans enjoyed the immense advantages given by radar. The flagship possessed only the SC type, which in any case Scott would not use since Intelligence sources had warned him that the Japanese now had receivers capable of detecting SC transmissions. *Helena* and *Boise*, however, were equipped with the new SG surface search radar, while the other vessels, including the destroyers, had gunnery control sets. Even earlier warning, Scott hoped, would be provided by the King-fisher seaplanes carried on each cruiser. At 2200, the signal was given for these to take to the air.

Despite Scott's efforts to increase his force's efficiency, he had not had enough time to eradicate those defects in communications which had so hampered the American ships previously. An early illustration of these was now given, for *Helena* never received the order to launch her Kingfisher. Remembering how such aircraft had proved a major fire hazard at Savo Island, Captain Gilbert Hoover wisely ordered it to be thrown overboard before the action commenced.

Nor did the scouts from the other cruisers prove of much value. That from *San Francisco* sent back a series of reports on a group of Japanese ships but unfortunately these were Joshima's not Goto's. *Boise*'s aircraft was forced to land near Savo Island by engine trouble. And the scout from *Salt Lake City* crashed in flames, having somehow ignited its own illumination flares.

This last mishap could have had dire consequences. The Japanese Bombardment Group was then 50 miles to the north-west, racing towards Scott at 26 knots. *Aoba* was in the lead, followed by *Furutaka*, then *Kinugasa*, with the destroyers on either beam of the flagship, *Hatsuyuki* to port and *Fubuki* to starboard. Goto had not brought his men to full readiness, believing that he had not yet reached the danger zone, but his astonishing lookouts, seeing the glare from the burning aircraft, gave the alarm. Goto, however, thought it was a signal from Joshima's convoy. *Aoba* therefore flashed a message which, not surprisingly, met with no response. The Japanese commander remained unconcerned. He had rashly assumed that after Savo Island the

Americans would never dare to engage at night.

At 2228, Scott, who had previously reduced speed to 20 knots, turned north-east. Although he was unaware of it, this move put his vessels in a perfect position, able to open fire simultaneously with full broadsides as they steered across the head of the hostile column, while only the front guns of the advancing ships would be able to reply; a tactic known for obvious reasons as 'Crossing the T'.

First contact with Goto's vessels was made by *Helena*'s radar at 2325. Captain Hoover, however, delayed reporting the sighting until he had had time to check that it was really of an enemy force. His caution was understandable but regrettable, for at 2332, Scott, deciding he had gone far enough to the north-east, determined to reverse course.

Oddly enough, Scott did not order each ship to turn in succession or all ships to turn together, either of which would have kept his force in its single line astern. Presumably he did not choose the latter course because it would have placed his flagship last of the four cruisers but it is difficult to see why he was reluctant to adopt the former manoeuvre, which in addition to preserving the tight control that he considered desirable, had the merit of simplicity.

Indeed there is some discussion as to exactly what action Scott did mean to take. Griffith has stated his belief that Scott wished the leading vessel in each division to turn simultaneously to port, with the other ships in the division following her round. This would result in destroyer *Buchanan* leading Task Force 64 back to the south-west, followed by destroyer *McCalla*, then the cruisers with *San Francisco* in front, then the other three destroyers headed by *Farenholt*.

If this was the intention, it can only be said that the order was misunderstood by both the van and the rear destroyers. It seems probable therefore that Scott did wish his ships to execute the manoeuvre they in fact adopted; namely all those behind the flagship were to follow her round in succession, while the three leading destroyers made an independent turn to port in succession, then increased speed so as to pass to starboard of the cruisers on their way to resume their original station at the head of the column. Morison remarks that 'there was nothing unusual in ordering this somewhat complicated procedure' but its use almost ruined all Scott's careful preparations for the coming combat.

US Aircraft Carrier *Wasp* torpedoed by Japanese Submarine *I-19*.

The end of USS *Wasp*.

Japanese Commanders:

Admiral Isoroku Yamamoto.

Rear-Admiral Raizo Tanaka.

Vice-Admiral Chuichi Nagumo.

Vice-Admiral Gunichi Mikawa.

Vice-Admiral Nobutake Kondo.

In the first place, as destroyer *Duncan* made her turn, she gained contact with the enemy on her gunnery radar set. Her skipper, Lieutenant-Commander Taylor, without informing Captain Tobin in *Farenholt*, gallantly though unwisely raced off to attack Goto's column single-handed. *Laffey*, astern, followed *Farenholt* but both were still in a perilous position between the rival cruisers when, at 2340, Captain Hoover, now certain that his radar contact was hostile, at last notified Scott. Shortly afterwards, light cruiser *Boise* also reported the enemy but so ambiguously that Scott did not know for certain that she was referring to the same force as *Helena*. Furthermore, she used the code-word 'bogies' which strictly speaking meant unidentified aircraft, not ships.

While Scott tried to clarify the situation, the range decreased to 5,000 yards. It had been intended that the American cruisers should open fire without waiting for orders but in view of the confusion prevailing, Captain Hoover felt obliged to ask for permission to do so. After an exchange of mutually misleading signals, he believed that he had obtained this.* At 2346, *Helena*'s 6-inch guns cracked out a full salvo which fell squarely on Goto's flagship *Aoba*. Only seconds later came the deeper roar of *Salt Lake City*'s 8-inch weapons; then *San Francisco*, *Boise*, *Farenholt* and *Laffey* all concentrated their fire on the hostile cruisers – as did *Duncan*, still closing in alone at 30 knots.

On this occasion it was the Japanese ships that were taken by surprise, with their guns trained fore and aft. *Furutaka* reacted with commendable promptness, putting a shell into *Salt Lake City* which killed several men. Rear-Admiral Goto, however, as his opponents had done at Savo Island, believed that a ghastly mistake had been made and he was being attacked by Joshima's force. He had time only to order his column to turn to starboard, when a series of well-placed salvoes struck both *Aoba* and *Furutaka*. On his shattered bridge, Goto collapsed mortally wounded and was carried to his sea cabin.

The Japanese were not the only ones who were confused about the identity of the ships which they were engaging. Only a minute after

---

* Hoover's enquiry over the TBS was 'Interrogatory Roger', which equalled: 'Request permission to open fire'. Yet, as is widely known, 'Roger' also means 'Message Received'. Scott thought Hoover was merely checking that an earlier sighting report had reached the flagship. His reply, 'Roger', was intended to convey: 'Confirmed your message received'. But it could also mean: 'Commence Firing'. Hoover read it in this sense and acted accordingly.

Helena had delivered the first salvo, Scott ordered 'Cease Fire', believing that Tobin's destroyers were being hit. He was able to ensure that *San Francisco* complied with his command but the gunners on the other ships turned deaf ears to it for several minutes. *Aoba*, already in flames, received more hits as she retired. *Furutaka*, while in the act of turning, was struck by several salvoes which knocked out her gun turrets and set her on fire as well, though she also managed to pull away to the north-west.

As the gunfire slowly died out, Scott called over the TBS to check whether the American destroyers had come under fire. Tobin confirmed that they had not, yet only when *Farenholt* and *Laffey* had flashed their coloured identification lights, was the Task Force commander sufficiently reassured to order 'Resume Firing' at 2351.

During this brief lull, *Aoba* and *Furutaka* attempted to escape but destroyer *Fubuki* on *Aoba*'s starboard beam did not alter course immediately and furthermore apparently shared Goto's belief that the vessels encountered were friendly, for she now switched on her identification lights. This attracted the unwelcome attention of *San Francisco*, which quickly turned a searchlight onto this new target. The wretched *Fubuki*, savaged by the gunfire of almost every ship in Task Force 64, was brought to a halt at 2353, exploded and sank.

In contrast, Captain Masao Sawa, skipper of heavy cruiser *Kinugasa* at the rear of Goto's column, seeing what had happened to his squadron-mates, wisely turned to port instead of following them. Destroyer *Hatsuyuki* did the same. This brought both vessels into conflict with *Duncan*. Lieutenant-Commander Taylor had been firing on *Furutaka* but now turned his guns on *Hatsuyuki*. Before they could do any harm, however, a shell, probably from *Kinugasa*, knocked out *Duncan*'s gun director. She continued firing on local control and launched a torpedo at *Furutaka*. Another salvo from *Kinugasa* then brought down *Duncan*'s forward stack and started fires. Nonetheless, she was still able to send a second torpedo at *Furutaka* which hit the enemy cruiser in the forward engine-room at 2354.

This was *Duncan*'s last act of defiance. Shells, many of them fired by the American cruisers which, not unnaturally, thought that *Duncan* was one of the enemy squadron, were falling all round her. A salvo from a 'friendly' vessel hit the engine-room (which had already been damaged earlier in the action), wrecked the radio, coding, radar plotting, gunnery plotting and interior communications rooms, and set the destroyer ablaze. Cut off by raging fires, Taylor and other personnel on the bridge had no choice but to take to a life raft, leaving their ship steaming in uncontrolled circles. The remainder of the crew continued the fight to save her but at 0200, by which time *Duncan* was engulfed in flames and shaken by exploding ammunition, they also were forced to abandon her, though she did not finally go down until shortly before noon. As at Savo Island, sharks took toll of the survivors but 195 officers and men out of an original complement of 243 were rescued at daybreak by destroyer *McCalla*.

Rear-Admiral Scott was of course unaware of *Duncan*'s troubles when, at 2355, he turned his Task Force north-west to pursue the retreating Japanese. In the course of this manoeuvre *Boise* was hit more than once, though she suffered little damage. It seems that she vented her wrath on the wrong target, for *Farenholt* was crippled by four 6-inch shells which probably came from *Boise*, as *Helena*, having tracked the enemy accurately for so long, would have been unlikely to have made the same mistake. One hit on the waterline knocked out the destroyer's communications as well as causing flooding, while another found her engine-room, releasing a cloud of scalding steam. *Farenholt*, however, was more fortunate than *Duncan*, since she was able to retire from the scene of combat at 20 knots.

The remaining American destroyers, *Laffey*, *Buchanan* and *McCalla*, joined their cruisers in firing at *Aoba* and *Furutaka*. *Buchanan* also directed five torpedoes at these targets, though without success. *Furutaka*, listing to port, with fires spreading and flooding increasing, was already doomed but *Aoba*, despite the punishment she had received, could still fight back, while *Kinugasa*, which had previously concentrated her attention on *Duncan*, was now preparing to engage Scott's cruisers.

Captain Sawa's intervention came at midnight, just as Scott ordered a temporary cease-fire. He quickly countermanded the order as a salvo from *Kinugasa* fell just astern of *San Francisco*. *Kinugasa* also fired torpedoes, which were narrowly avoided by *Boise*.

Shortly thereafter, *Boise*'s radar warned of a target to starboard. She turned on a searchlight to illuminate this; then opened fire. Unfortunately the searchlight beam gave the Japanese gunners a clear point of aim. *Aoba* – for such was the enemy vessel – scored four hits. Then *Kinugasa* joined in with devastating effect. An 8-inch shell entered *Boise*'s forward gun turret where it exploded. Another burst through her thin hull below the waterline, detonating the forward magazine. A huge column of orange flame rose high above the ship. Though Captain Moran ordered the magazine flooded, no one remained alive to obey him; but mercifully sea water, which was pouring through the gap torn by the shell, quenched the flames in time to preserve *Boise* from almost certain destruction.

The shattered light cruiser was protected from further harm by Captain Small of *Salt Lake City* who gallantly steered his ship between *Boise* and *Kinugasa*. This enabled *Boise*, at 0012, to turn hard to port out of the action. Her casualties were 107 dead, 35 wounded, but her damage control parties, who had to master both fires and flooding, saved the ship; though she had to leave the combat zone, ultimately going as far as Philadelphia to effect repairs.

Salt Lake City continued her duel with *Kinugasa* for a time, the American cruiser receiving two hits, the Japanese cruiser four. Neither was much damaged. The Japanese also covered their withdrawal by firing torpedoes, though without result. At 0020, Rear-Admiral Scott, who, like Mikawa at Savo Island, thought he had done enough for one night, ordered his force to cease fire; then at 0028, to turn away to the south-west.

The remnants of the Bombardment Group certainly had no intention of resuming hostilities. *Furutaka* finally capsized and sank at about 0040. *Aoba*, though still capable of 20 knots, had been savaged by 40 shell hits. Captain Kikunori Kijima, the Chief of Staff, leaned over the mortally wounded Goto to whisper: 'Die satisfied Admiral. We have sunk two enemy cruisers.' Escaping unscathed from an attack by Henderson Field's aircraft at 0700, the remaining Japanese ships retired to their advance base at Shortland Island, whence *Aoba* had to return to Japan for major repairs. The luckless Captain Kijima was promptly relieved of his command by Vice-Admiral Mikawa.

Under cover of the clash between the cruiser groups, Rear-Admiral Joshima had successfully landed his troops, supplies and heavy artillery. He then retired, but in the early hours of 12th October, having learned what had happened, he detached two destroyers, *Shirayuki* and *Murakumo*, to look for survivors from *Furutaka* and *Fubuki*. They had rescued about 400 men when aircraft from

Henderson Field made their appearance. The destroyers survived the first raid with minor damage but at 0800, under cover of a strafing attack by fourteen Wildcats, six Dauntless dive-bombers made three near-misses on *Murakumo*. Next a flight of six torpedo-carrying Avengers led by Lieutenant Larsen (formerly of *Saratoga*) scored a direct hit on *Murakumo*'s port side which brought her to a halt amid a cloud of smoke and steam. She had to be scuttled later.

By early afternoon, another of Joshima's destroyers, *Natsugumo*, had joined *Shirayuki*. At 1645, Lieutenant-Commander Eldridge led ten Dauntlesses against them, personally making a bomb hit on *Natsugumo* amidships, while two of his pilots recorded near-misses. A huge explosion shook *Natsugumo*; she slowly rolled over and sank soon afterwards.

There is no doubt that the United States Navy won the Battle of Cape Esperance, even if claims that Task Force 64 had sunk four cruisers and four destroyers were somewhat optimistic. Yet, bearing in mind the advantage conferred on them by radar, the Americans' final achievement must be considered rather disappointing. Furthermore because of Scott's victory, it was felt that his long, inflexible single-column formation was correct. It was adopted on later occasions with regrettable results. Nor was it appreciated that the Japanese had been unusually unwary in this instance. In particular, they had been unable to make their traditional torpedo attack at the start of the action – a state of affairs that would not be repeated.

However, if the battle lacked decisive results, its moral effects were very great. The confidence of the Japanese seamen was badly shaken. For them the realization that radar was able to disclose their movements long before even the finest of lookouts could discover the least trace of an enemy, cast a dark shadow over the future.

In contrast, the Americans' morale was raised dramatically. For the first time they lost that feeling of inferiority which had previously haunted them in operations at night. And as they became more practised in the use of radar, their new-found optimism would become ever more justified.

No one, either at the time or later, appears to have noticed how appropriate was the name of the headland after which the action became known. Esperance. Cape Hope.

CHAPTER FIVE

The Battle of Santa Cruz

The air of confidence among the Americans increased on the evening of 12th October, when minesweepers *Hovey* and *Southard* reached Tulagi, towing four PT-boats:— *PT-38*, *PT-46*, *PT-48* and *PT-60*. These motor-torpedo-boats had no protection whatever against shell-fire but they could reach a speed of 40 knots, which, together with their considerable manoeuvrability, would, it was hoped, enable them to pose a threat to the 'Tokyo Expresses', at least under cover of darkness.

Far greater encouragement was given early next morning when Rear-Admiral Turner's transports set ashore the soldiers of the 164th Infantry regiment, with their supplies, ammunition, vehicles and anti-tank guns. They then embarked the survivors of the 1st Raider Battalion and retired unscathed.

It was as well that American morale had been raised for the Japanese had devised a plan which they were certain would provide a 'final solution' to the problem of re-capturing Guadalcanal. Rightly regarding American command of the skies as a crucial factor, they intended first to neutralize Henderson Field with bombardments from the air, from the sea and from the new artillery pieces – the 'Pistol Petes' – so recently landed by Rear-Admiral Joshima. At the same time they would supply a final batch of reinforcements to Lieutenant-General Hyakutake, while a powerful fleet which had left Truk on 11th October under the command of Vice-Admiral Kondo, would take up station north of the Solomons to prevent the Americans bringing in any reinforcements of their own.

With the 'Cactus Air Force' destroyed, Hyakutake's soldiers would break through the defences to seize the airfield and its neighbouring food, fuel and ammunition dumps. To Major-General Tadashi Sumiyoshi was entrusted the task of striking over the sand-bar at the mouth of the Matanikau River. At the same time a force under

Colonel Oka would ford it about a mile and a half upstream so as to take the defenders in the flank.

These advances, however, were intended mainly to distract American attention from Lieutenant-General Maruyama's Second Division which would make the main thrust against the vital 'Bloody Ridge' at the south of the perimeter. 'X-Day' or to be more exact night, on which Maruyama's attacks would commence, was provisionally fixed for 22nd October.

Once Henderson Field had been secured, Kondo would move south. The pilots of two of his carriers, *Hiyo* and *Junyo*, who were comparatively inexperienced, would fly their aircraft to Guadalcanal to provide close support; those from *Shokaku*, *Zuikaku* and light carrier *Zuiho* would prevent all attempts to evacuate Vandegrift's men by sea; and a small transport unit would carry a detachment of troops to Koli Point, east of the American lines, to cut off any retreat by land.

The first part of the plan went well. At 1202 on 13th October, 27 Bettys, guarded by eighteen Zeros, made a highly accurate attack which inflicted the first casualties on the 164th Infantry Regiment. At 1350, while the Wildcats were refuelling, eighteen more Bettys, with a similar fighter escort, devastated the airfield. Then the Japanese heavy artillery joined in. While the Seabees strove to fill the craters, destroyers *Sterett*, *Gwin* and *Nicholas* shelled the enemy positions – but the 'Pistol Petes' kept on firing.

Neither bombs nor artillery-fire, however, prepared the Americans for their next ordeal. That night, Vice-Admiral Takeo Kurita entered Ironbottom Sound with battleships *Kongo* (flagship) and *Haruna*, escorted by light cruiser *Isuzu*, flying the flag of the ubiquitous Rear-Admiral Tanaka, and six destroyers. In their magazines, the 'battlewagons' had over 900 14-inch shells, 300 of which were the high-explosive type, designed specifically to inflict casualties on men or aircraft.

At about 0100 on 14th October, Japanese seaplanes dropped brilliant flares over the airfield. The great guns on *Kongo* and *Haruna* thundered. The 'recce' aircraft signalled fall of shot. Gunnery officers corrected angles of fire. A second salvo was followed by great flames rising high above the landing-strip. The battleships began firing continuously, while Tanaka's destroyers closed in to pour their 5-inch shells into the fires. These spread slowly until they covered the entire airfield, above which hung a cloud of scattered debris.

There was little that the Americans could do except take cover. *Kongo* and *Haruna* were well out of range of the shore-batteries. The four PT-boats from Tulagi made a spirited attempt to torpedo them but without success. It was not, however, without value, for Kurita, well satisfied with the effects of his bombardment, decided it was pointless to risk damage by prolonging his visit. At 0230, he ordered his vessels to retire.

Dawn revealed a scene of desolation. The runway was pitted with craters, its steel matting thrown over hundreds of yards. Most of Vandegrift's aviation fuel, much of his ammunition and many of his bombs had been destroyed. 48 of his aircraft had been wrecked or crippled, including sixteen Wildcats, all his torpedo-planes and all except seven of his Dauntlesses. Supply dumps had also been hit; the hospital badly damaged; the radio station demolished. Amazingly there were only some 60 casualties but 41 of these were fatal, among them the commanding officer, Major Bell, and four other pilots from Marine Squadron 141, a dive-bomber unit that had reached the island on 23rd September. For the rest of the war, Guadalcanal veterans would refer to this ordeal as '*The* Bombardment'.

That the raid shook the defenders is obvious, although whether their morale was quite as ravaged as most authorities make out may be questioned, if only from an incident mentioned by Thomas G. Miller Jnr. in his book *The Cactus Air Force*, showing the reaction of one fighter pilot, Lieutenant Danny Doyle,* after the shelling had lasted about an hour. By this time, as Miller reports:

A nearby gasoline dump was spouting roaring flames hundreds of feet high, parked planes were blazing all over Henderson Field, an ammunition depot was cooking off with spectacular display and flares drifted down periodically from Japanese aircraft flying overhead. When a temporary lull in the noise came, Doyle leaned over and inquired of one of his neighbours: 'Say, do you think it would reveal our position if I lit a cigarette?'

* Killed in action, alas, on 7th November 1942.

The morning of the 14th brought renewed artillery-fire, while at 1206, 26 Bettys bombed Henderson Field without opposition since the surviving American aircraft had been moved to the 'cow pasture' – the fighter strip. When another eighteen Bettys arrived about an hour later, however, the Wildcats put up such a staunch resistance that the Japanese bombers, despite the protection of fifteen Zeros, were driven off without inflicting serious damage.

Meanwhile two of the remaining Dauntlesses had taken off to scout to the north-west. They were dismayed to sight six transports, guarded by eight destroyers, carrying Hyakutake's reinforcements. A raid by four dive-bombers plus a handful of P-400s armed with bombs was directed against this convoy but achieved only near-misses on destroyer *Samidare*.

Rear-Admiral Tamotsu Takama, commanding the reinforcement mission, proceeded unperturbed. Soon afterwards his men were able to cheer Vice-Admiral Mikawa who led heavy cruisers *Chokai* and *Kinugasa*, accompanied by two destroyers, at full speed past the convoy on the way to deliver another bombardment. That night 752 8-inch shells fell on Henderson Field.

Under cover of Mikawa's attack, the transports arrived off Tassafaronga. By dawn on 15th October, they had disembarked their troops as well as half their cargoes – food, equipment, ammunition and medical supplies. They continued unloading in daylight, confident that the 'Cactus Air Force' would be unable to interfere. It was a big mistake. Refuelled and re-armed from hidden reserves, every aircraft on Guadalcanal that could fly struck at the landing-area. By mid-morning twin-engined Douglas Dakotas began to arrive from Espiritu Santo carrying more precious aviation fuel. Fighting their way past patrolling Zeros – six of which they shot down – the Americans continued their raids almost without pause. Major Cram, flying a Catalina, added two torpedoes to the weapons used. Flying Fortresses from Espiritu Santo joined in the assault.

At a cost of three dive-bombers and four fighters, the 'Cactus Air Force' so damaged three Japanese transports – *Azumasan Maru*, *Kyushu Maru* and *Sasako Maru* – that they were forced to beach, ultimately becoming total losses. At 1550, Takama wisely decided to withdraw his remaining vessels all of which had suffered at least some damage.

Nonetheless, the soldiers together with about 80 per cent of their supplies had got ashore. Hyakutake now had under his command about 22,000 men, a large proportion of them fresh troops, to oppose 23,000 Americans – plus 4,500 more on Tulagi – a third of whom were suffering from malnutrition, dysentery, malaria or plain exhaustion.

Nor were the Japanese prevented from mounting successful strikes of their own. Their reconnaissance aircraft reported an American convoy consisting of cargo-ships *Alchiba* and *Bellatrix*, motor torpedo boat tender *Jamestown*, tug *Vireo*, and destroyers *Nicholas* and *Meredith*, each towing a barge laden with bombs and aviation fuel. Realizing that they had been sighted, all these vessels retired to Espiritu Santo except *Meredith* and *Vireo*. They also turned back after an ineffective air raid at 1050. About noon, Lieutenant-Commander Hubbard, *Meredith*'s skipper, decided that the slow, vulnerable *Vireo* would have to be abandoned. He took off her crew but just as he was about to torpedo her, 27 aircraft from Kondo's carriers appeared overhead. In one swift attack they burst through *Meredith*'s AA fire, to sink her almost instantaneously.

Vireo was not harmed but she was drifting away so rapidly that only one life-raft managed to reach her. The men from this were saved when the tug was salvaged later. The other rafts were only sighted after three days and three nights had passed, by which time 51 sailors from *Vireo* and 185 from *Meredith* had died, including Hubbard who was only one of many to fall victim to sharks.

Further unpleasantness occurred that night, when heavy cruisers *Myoko* and *Maya* entered Ironbottom Sound, escorted by a group of destroyers. Commencing at about midnight, 800 8-inch shells and 300 5-inch shells rained upon Henderson Field, setting fuel dumps alight, destroying fifteen Wildcats and damaging many other aircraft.

Yet the following day (16th October) saw the Americans doggedly bringing in further supplies. The aerial transports continued to provide aviation fuel, though each could carry only enough to keep twelve Wildcats aloft for about an hour. Seaplane-tender *McFarland* arrived with ammunition, twelve torpedoes and 40,000 gallons of fuel. That evening she was attacked by nine Val dive-bombers. Her AA gunners shot down one but another scored a direct hit on a barge which was alongside taking off the last of her fuel, turning it into an inferno, while yet another put a bomb on her depth-charge racks which blew off her rudder, damaged her port engine, killed 27 of her crew and wounded 28 more.

Shortly before, the nineteen Wildcats of Marine Squadron 212, led by Lieutenant-Colonel Harold Bauer, had landed at Henderson Field. When the raiders were sighted, Bauer, his fighter hastily refuelled, took off again alone. He was too late to prevent the strike on *McFarland* but avenged her misfortunes by downing four more Vals. The sea-plane-tender was towed to Tulagi by *YP-239*. Next day she moved up the Maliali River on Florida Island, where her crew carried out repairs. Three weeks later, she was able to start the return journey to Espiritu Santo.

Early on the morning of 17th October, destroyers *Aaron Ward* and *Lardner* shelled enemy positions, only to become in turn targets for eighteen bomb-carrying Kates, escorted by the same number of Zeros. Luckily, however, American code-breakers had learned the details of this raid beforehand, so eight Wildcats were already in position to attack the Japanese from above; they shot down six bombers and four fighters for the loss of one of their own number.

The 'Cactus Air Force' had more successes on 18th October, destroying three Bettys and four Zeros at a cost of two Wildcats whose pilots escaped by parachute. The same day also saw work begun on a new fighter strip which, when completed early in November, would be out of range of enemy artillery. The day's most dramatic event, however, took place well away from the combat zone.

It will be recalled that Admiral Nimitz had visited Guadalcanal at the end of September. He had then flown to New Caledonia where Ghormley's seemingly perennial pessimism had left a most unfavourable impression. As the crisis in early October worsened, Ghormley's gloomy messages convinced Nimitz that 'a tougher leader was needed'. On 18th October, Vice-Admiral William Halsey, who was on a tour of inspection preparatory to taking command of a carrier task force, reached Noumea. He was greeted with a signal appointing him Commander, South Pacific forthwith. With feelings of 'astonishment, apprehension and regret in that order', Halsey replaced a man who was his old personal friend.

Nimitz could scarcely have selected a more pugnacious officer. Halsey had come late to naval aviation, having been awarded his

'wings' in 1934 at the age of 52. Yet during the first six months of
hostilities, he had commanded so many carrier-strikes against enemy
bases – including the famous raid by Lieutenant-Colonel Doolittle's
Mitchell bombers on Tokyo – that his name had become virtually
synonymous with this form of warfare.*

Halsey's greatest value to his country, however, lay in the field of
morale. His confident personality was inspiring. His popularity among
thousands of sailors who had never even seen him was astonishing.
Called 'Bill' by his friends, he quickly become 'The Bull' to the news-
papers. Although nobody who knew him ever referred to him by this
nickname, it somehow symbolized the figure he presented to the world
of the aggressive, impulsive, determined fighter. The announcement of
his appointment was received with delighted cheers throughout the
South Pacific.

Yet although Halsey summoned Turner and Vandegrift to a conference at Noumea on the 23rd, where he promised them every possible support, in practice, like his predecessor, he was quite unable to
provide any additional aid to the Guadalcanal garrison or the 'Cactus
Air Force' in the desperate days which lay immediately ahead; or to
influence the course of the savage land-actions which were just beginning to develop.

Nor did Halsey correct existing tactical or strategic weaknesses. One
of the complaints against Ghormley had been that he allowed too
many ships to risk the perils of 'Torpedo Junction'. Halsey made no
attempt to rectify this situation with the result that the first important
incident of his term of command was the torpedoing by *I-176* of
heavy cruiser *Chester* which was operating with a task group in this
area on 20th October; she had to return to Norfolk, Virginia for
repairs. Even then it was not until torpedoes from *I-15* narrowly missed
battleship *Washington* on the 27th, that Halsey was convinced of the
follies of keeping such important vessels continuously at sea in
submarine-infested waters.

Furthermore Halsey had one great defect which weakened all his
virtues. 'He hated the enemy,' says Morison, 'with an unholy wrath.'
His reported comment when he heard of the attack on Pearl Harbor,
that after the war the Japanese language would be spoken only in

* Only a skin disease which had put him on the sick-list had prevented Halsey
from commanding the American carriers at Midway.

hell – even if the story grew in the telling – adequately sums up his attitude.

And because Halsey loathed his enemy, he came to despise him. He prophesied victory as early as 1943. Later he would claim that he had known his statement 'could not possibly be true. I wanted to exaggerate as the Japanese exaggerate to break down their morale.' Yet it is difficult to avoid the conclusion that the real reason for his opinion was that contempt for his foes made him over-estimate the prospects of success against them. It was a dangerous attitude which would lead to unnecessary perils.

In retrospect therefore, it seems that the main importance of Halsey's appointment was that by selecting him, Nimitz served notice on both friend and foe that however long or hard the Guadalcanal campaign might be, the Americans would see it through to the bitter end.

*

Bitter indeed was the fighting that now commenced for Henderson Field. Starting on 20th October, Major-General Sumiyoshi had made a series of probing attacks on the lower Matanikau. On the 21st, destroyer *Nicholas*, which had just escorted a small convoy to the island, effectively bombarded enemy positions but Sumiyoshi persisted, thereby drawing the full attention of the Americans, who were quite unaware of the threat from Maruyama's Second Division, making its way towards the 'Bloody Ridge'.

Yet once again, the Japanese had ignored the difficulties of moving through the appalling jungle. One after another, Maruyama's artillery pieces had to be abandoned. His infantrymen pushed on doggedly. 'During this march', Griffith reports, 'Japanese soldiers, subsisting on nothing more than a few handfuls of rice softened to edible consistency by rain water, again demonstrated their unequaled qualities of tenacity and endurance.' For all their efforts, however, it was soon clear that they could not reach their attack positions on 22nd October as planned. Maruyama reluctantly postponed his assault for 24 hours.

By the morning of the 23rd, Maruyama's left wing under Major-General Yumio Nasu was ready for its final advance on the still unsuspecting Americans. The right wing, however, which was led by

Major-General Kawaguchi – who had already had one failure in this same area – was still struggling through the jungle. Postponing his attack once more to the 24th, the infuriated Maruyama directed Colonel Shoji to take over command from Kawaguchi, who was then ordered back to Japan where he was placed on the Reserve List.

For some reason news of the latest postponement never reached the Japanese troops on the lower Matanikau. Sumiyoshi was down with malaria but his officers advanced across the sandspit at the river's mouth a few minutes after 1800 on 23rd October, as previously planned. The Americans, anticipating trouble in this area, had brought up a heavy artillery concentration which smashed the assault, killing some 600 of the attackers. The defenders' only heavy loss was in expenditure of ammunition. Next day, the Douglas Dakotas made good the deficiency.

Admiral Yamamoto was now seriously concerned about the delay in capturing the airfield. Already on the 22nd, one of Kondo's carriers, *Hiyo*, had had to return to Truk with engine trouble, escorted by destroyers *Isonami* and *Inadzuma*, while her aircraft were flown to Rabaul to replace recent heavy losses. On the 24th, Yamamoto bluntly warned that unless Henderson Field was taken quickly the fleet would have to withdraw due to shortage of fuel.

Thus pressed, Maruyama prepared to deliver his assault that night. Unfortunately, not only had Shoji's right wing still not come up but during the day Nasu's left wing had at last been spotted. When the Japanese advanced shortly after midnight, the defenders were ready.

The fighting followed the same pattern as at the 'Tenaru' and the 'Bloody Ridge'. Once more the Marines, commanded on this occasion by Lieutenant-Colonel Puller, reinforced by a battalion of the 164th Infantry under Lieutenant-Colonel Hall, broke every attack with mortar and machine-gun fire. When morning came, the Japanese sullenly fell back to regroup leaving more than enough bodies behind to justify the name of 'Coffin Corner' being given to this section of the defences.

Furthermore, in the course of the action, Maruyama received a false report that his troops had broken through to Henderson Field. Without waiting for confirmation, he signalled the good news to Hyakutake, who in turn passed it on to his naval colleagues.

One of the officers thus misinformed was Vice-Admiral Mikawa, who accordingly ordered destroyers *Akatsuki*, *Ikazuchi* and *Shiratsuyu* to set off with the troops for Koli Point, and Rear-Admiral Takama with light cruiser *Yura* and destroyers *Akitsuki*, *Yudachi*, *Harusame*, *Murasame* and *Samidare* to cover them by yet another bombardment. So poor was the co-operation between the Japanese services, however, that these vessels were not warned of the correct situation even after it became known to the Imperial Army.

Nevertheless when the destroyers carrying the 'Koli Detachment' first entered Ironbottom Sound, no American aircraft could take off to oppose them since heavy rains had flooded the air-strips. The only warships on hand were *Trever* and *Zane*, two destroyer-minesweepers of World War I vintage, which had just towed four new PT-boats to, and unloaded a supply of torpedoes, fuel and ammunition at, the base at Tulagi. They had no chance in combat against three modern Japanese destroyers, so when these were sighted at about 1000, *Trever* and *Zane* fled to the east. The enemy turned in pursuit. At 1038, a hit on *Zane* killed three men, wounded nine and knocked out a gun.

By this time, however, the sun had dried out the 'cow pasture' sufficiently to allow three Wildcats to get airborne. These now hurtled out of the sun in a strafing attack that caused little damage but immense consternation to the Japanese destroyers whose crews were thus made aware that the airfields had not after all been occupied by their ground-forces.

Accordingly *Akatsuki*, *Ikazuchi* and *Shiratsuyu*, abandoning their chase of the destroyer-minesweepers, steered towards Guadalcanal. Here they sighted tug *Seminole* and *YP-284* both of which they promptly sank. They then engaged shore-batteries at Lunga Point, but at 1055, *Akatsuki* received a hit from the return fire that convinced the enemy that the time had come to retire – which they did under cover of a smoke-screen.

Meanwhile the main body of the 'Cactus Air Force' had been able to take off. This was fortunate, for Takama's bombardment unit was still intent on carrying out its mission. At 1255, five Dauntless dive-bombers led by Lieutenant-Commander Eldridge attacked these vessels, Eldridge hitting light cruiser *Yura* on her forecastle with a 500-pound bomb, while his pilots caused more damage to *Yura* and also to destroyer *Akitsuki* by near-misses.

The proposed bombardment was cancelled forthwith as Takama

turned north to escape but the Henderson Field airmen were relent-
less. At 1420, fighter-bombers near-missed *Yura* twice more. At 1500,
a Dauntless near-missed her again while another near-missed *Akitsuki*.
About an hour and a half later, *Akitsuki* was further damaged by
another near-miss, while *Yura* was set on fire and crippled by a direct
hit. At 1700, the light cruiser received the final blow from a flight of
six Flying Fortresses. Destroyers *Yudachi* and *Harusame* took off her
survivors; then finished her off with torpedoes.

While these attacks were in progress, American fighters were grap-
pling with a series of air raids on Henderson Field. They undoubtedly
shot down six Zeros and so badly damaged three more that these failed
to return to base. They also claimed five Bettys. Enemy records make
no mention of bomber losses but it seems that they must be in-
complete; one of the Bettys at least definitely crashed less than a mile
from the airfield. Only one Wildcat was lost in combat, though ten
others received some degree of damage, mainly in accidents taking-off
or landing on the still treacherous surfaces.

At the end of the day the 'Cactus Air Force' possessed twelve Wildcats, eleven Dauntlesses and six fighter-bombers still in a condition to
be flown by the exhausted pilots. Yet no more enemy raids were made
for five days – and then only half-a-dozen strafing Zeros appeared.
Japan's Eleventh Air Fleet had been fatally weakened by its losses of
the previous fortnight. Never again would it break through the
American defences by sheer weight of numbers. Henderson Field
would never now be neutralized by air-attacks.

On the other hand, the bombing raids had prevented the Americans
turning their attention to Maruyama who was preparing for a 'final
death-defying night attack', in which Colonel Shoji's men were now
ready to join. At 2200, both Japanese columns began a furious assault.
When it was defeated, the enemy withdrew, reorganized, tried again.
Seven separate attacks were made that night. They resulted only in
a ghastly slaughter.

By dawn, the Sendai Division, with half its officers including Major-
General Nasu dead, could do no more. Maruyama ordered Shoji's
troops to strike eastward to Koli Point but the remainder of his command began a slow retirement westward. In the early hours of the
26th, the diversionary Japanese assault on the upper Matanikau,
which had been delayed by terrain terrible even for Guadalcanal, was

Japanese Transport *Kyushu Maru* wrecked on Guadalcanal, 15th October 1942.

Japanese Aircraft Carrier *Shokaku.*

The Battle of Santa Cruz: Attack on US Aircraft Carrier *Hornet*.

The Battle of Santa Cruz: Attack on US Aircraft Carrier *Enterprise*.

at last launched. After an initial success, it was thrown back with heavy losses by a counter-attack of communications personnel, company runners and cooks – one of whom, rumour insisted, felled a Japanese officer with a pancake.

American casualties in this series of actions amounted to some 200 Marines or soldiers killed, another 200 wounded – surprisingly light when the fury of the attacks is considered. The Japanese dead alone reached about 3,500. Further reinforcements would have to be brought in before the enemy could take the offensive again.

So 26th October began looking very well for the Americans. The air-attacks on their base had failed. The ground-attacks on their base had failed. Submarine *Amberjack* arrived to ease the supply problem by delivering 1,000 gallons of aviation fuel and 10 tons of bombs.* At sea also it appeared that all was going satisfactorily. A Catalina from Espiritu Santo had sighted Kondo's ships on the 23rd and that night Rear-Admiral Aubrey Fitch – who on 20th September had relieved McCain in command of the land-based aircraft in the South Pacific – sent other Catalinas to attack them; unfortunately without results. On the 25th, Flying Fortresses made near-misses on battleship *Kirishima*, though she escaped damage. On the night of the 25/26th, a Catalina dropped two bombs very close to *Zuikaku*, while another hit destroyer *Isokaze* with a torpedo which regrettably did not explode.

This series of incidents so alarmed Kondo that at about 0400 on 26th October, his entire fleet reversed course to the north. The Japanese master-plan had finally been abandoned.

*

Yet at the precise moment that the Americans had in practice gained the upper hand on, and in the skies above Guadalcanal – though they were not then fully aware of this – they experienced a sharp, if luckily indecisive defeat at sea : the Battle of Santa Cruz.

It was a defeat made the more unpalatable by being quite unnecessary. When Halsey had succeeded Ghormley, only one US carrier, *Hornet*, remained in the South Pacific. Nimitz, however, had

---

* The submarine had reached Ironbottom Sound on the previous day, having a 'fish-eye' view of the naval encounters already described. Because of the nature of her cargo, she had wisely waited until all immediate dangers had passed.

ensured that the repairs required by *Enterprise* after the Eastern
Solomons were completed in the shortest possible time. On 26th
October, accompanied by the new, fast battleship *South Dakota*, she
also joined Halsey's command.

The combined carrier groups, which were placed under the tactical
control of Rear-Admiral Thomas Kinkaid, could well have remained
on the defensive. Had they done so and had the Japanese fleet continued its advance, Kinkaid would have been aided by the aircraft at
Henderson Field when he engaged it. In practice, as has been seen,
Vice-Admiral Kondo had no intention of advancing at all until the
Imperial Army had secured the air-strips.

Unfortunately Halsey scorned defensive fighting. 'I believe in violat-
ing the rules,' he once remarked. 'We violate them every day.'
Heedless of the disaster that would result from the loss of America's
last two serviceable carriers, he ordered them off to attack Kondo.
That Halsey came to appreciate he had taken an unjustified risk is
shown by his observation after the battle that he would never again
let the enemy 'suck' his 'flat-tops' to the north.

How great a risk Halsey was running can be seen from an examina-
tion of the rival fleets. At dawn on 26th October, the American vessels
were some 125 miles north of the Santa Cruz Islands, heading north-
westward at 20 knots towards the Japanese, then less than 200 miles
distant. As at the Eastern Solomons, they formed two separate groups
about ten miles apart, each centred on one of the carriers.

Of these, the group guarding *Enterprise*, in which Kinkaid flew his
flag, was somewhat the stronger, consisting of battleship *South Dakota*,
generously equipped with new 40-mm anti-aircraft guns, heavy cruiser
Portland, light cruiser *San Juan* and destroyers *Porter*, *Mahan*,
Cushing, *Preston*, *Smith*, *Maury*, *Conyngham* and *Shaw*. *Hornet*, the
flagship of Rear-Admiral George Murray, was protected by heavy
cruisers *Northampton* and *Pensacola*, light cruisers *San Diego* and
Juneau and destroyers *Morris*, *Anderson*, *Hughes*, *Mustin*, *Russell* and
Barton.

It may be mentioned that Halsey also had another task force under
his command, made up of battleship *Washington*, heavy cruiser *San
Francisco*, light cruisers *Helena* and *Atlanta* and six destroyers. These,
however, had been sent to operate independently in the vicinity of
Guadalcanal. It was a pity that Halsey had not instructed them to join

Kinkaid for though they would not have seen a surface action, their AA guns would have proved of immense value.

Even if the *Washington* group had reinforced him, Kinkaid would still have been out-numbered by Kondo's fleet, which, as at the Eastern Solomons, was divided into a number of widely separated formations. Nearest to the Americans was the Vanguard Group. Commanded by Rear-Admiral Abe, it contained battleships *Hiei* and *Kirishima*, heavy cruisers *Tone*, *Chikuma* and *Suzuya*, light cruiser *Nagara* and destroyers *Kazegumo*, *Makigumo*, *Yugumo*, *Akigumo*, *Tanikaze*, *Urakaze* and *Isokaze*.

About 60 miles further north steamed the Striking Force of Vice-Admiral Nagumo, who flew his flag in carrier *Shokaku*. She was accompanied by her inseparable partner, carrier *Zuikaku*, together with light carrier *Zuiho*. Protection was provided by heavy cruiser *Kumano* and destroyers *Amatsukaze*, *Hatsukaze*, *Tokitsukaze*, *Yukikaze*, *Maikaze*, *Hamakaze*, *Arashi* and *Terutsuki*.

A further 120 miles to the north-west was Kondo's own group which although bringing up the rear of the Japanese fleet, was somewhat oddly entitled the Advance Force. Kondo had under his immediate control battleships *Kongo* (flagship of Vice-Admiral Kurita) and *Haruna*, heavy cruisers *Atago* (his own flagship), *Takao*, *Myoko* and *Maya*, light cruiser *Isuzu* (flagship of Rear-Admiral Tanaka), and twelve destroyers: *Naganami*, *Makinami*, *Takanami*, *Umikaze*, *Kawakaze*, *Suzukaze*, *Oyashio*, *Kagero*, *Murasame*, *Harusame*, *Samidare* and *Yudachi*.

Finally to the west of Kondo was stationed Rear-Admiral Kakuji Kakuta with carrier *Junyo*, screened by destroyers *Kuroshio* and *Hayashio*.

Kondo's superiority in aircraft was not so great but he could deploy 87 fighters, 68 dive-bombers and 57 torpedo-planes, whereas Kinkaid had originally controlled 70 Wildcats, 72 Dauntlesses and only 29 Avengers. Furthermore on the 25th, after receiving a contact report from one of Fitch's Catalinas (which had then lost touch in a rainstorm), *Enterprise* had sent out twelve scouts at 1330, followed by eighteen dive-bombers and eleven fighters at 1420. When these returned in darkness after a vain search, the first one back crashed on landing. This caused a delay before the other aircraft could be brought down, as a result of which six of them were forced to ditch by lack

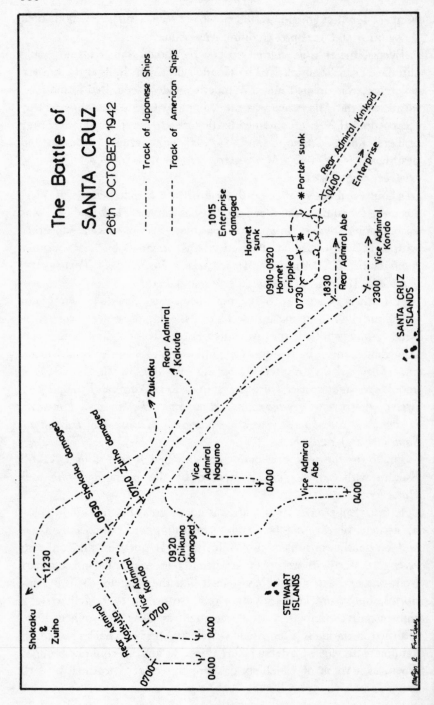

The Battle of
SANTA CRUZ
26th OCTOBER 1942

---·---·--- Track of Japanese Ships

------------- Track of American Ships

of fuel – a hard blow for the weaker fleet to suffer.

This incident was indicative of a further American disadvantage. *Enterprise* carried a new Air Group – the first to have been formed since Pearl Harbor – in which the majority of the pilots were very inexperienced, having only just completed their training. To make matters worse, Halsey, who had flown his flag in *Enterprise* earlier in the war, had deprived her of a number of key personnel including her fighter-director officer, whom he had taken to serve on his staff at Noumea.

Soon after 0300 on the night of 25/26th October, one of the Catalinas which had been searching for Kondo sent in a report of 'a large carrier and six other vessels'. Unhappily this message did not reach Kinkaid, via Fitch's HQ at Espiritu Santo, until 0512, by which time he had already sent off sixteen of *Enterprise's* Dauntlesses, each armed with a 500-pound bomb, on an armed reconnaissance. Distrusting the reliability of a sighting made at night and recalling how the Americans had sent their main attack against a diversionary unit at the Eastern Solomons, Kinkaid, understandably if unfortunately, decided to wait for information from his own scouts before launching a striking force.

At 0617, two of the 'recce' aircraft – for they were flying in pairs – spotted Abe's Vanguard Group* but not until 0650, were Nagumo's carriers sighted. The successful pilots, Lieutenant-Commander Lee and Ensign Johnson, broadcast their news, then tried to make a bombing run – only to be engaged by Zeros. After shooting down three of these, they managed to escape into convenient cloud-cover.

On receipt of this information, Kinkaid made preparations for action but unhappily these did not proceed smoothly. At 0730, fifteen dive-bombers, six Avengers armed with torpedoes and eight Wildcats took off from *Hornet*. To save time and fuel, they set out forthwith instead of waiting for the inexperienced airmen from *Enterprise*, from which three dive-bombers, eight torpedo-planes and eight Wildcats were launched only at 0800. These were followed at 0815, by a second strike of nine Dauntlesses, nine Avengers armed with bombs and seven fighters from *Hornet*.

The Japanese were quicker off the mark. At 0630, one of their re-

---

* Later other scouts from *Enterprise* also located Abe's vessels and made ineffective attacks on heavy cruiser *Tone*.

connaissance aircraft sighted *Hornet*. At 0710, twenty Vals from *Shokaku*, eighteen Kates from *Zuikaku*, eighteen Zeros from *Zuikaku* and nine Zeros from *Zuiho* left on their mission of destruction.

Preparations were then begun for another raid but at 0740, long before this could be made ready, two of *Enterprise*'s scouts, piloted by Lieutenant Strong and Ensign Irvine, dived upon *Zuiho*, their bombs striking her near the stern, knocking out her after AA batteries, starting fires and tearing a jagged 50-foot hole in her flight-deck that prevented Captain Obayashi from joining in any further flying operations. The light carrier had previously sent up Zeros on combat air patrol. Furious and humiliated, these chased Strong and Irvine for miles but the Americans made good their escape, downing two of their pursuers for good measure.

Nagumo accepted the blow stoically. By 0822, his second strike – twenty Vals from *Zuikaku* and twelve Kates and twelve Zeros from *Shokaku* – was airborne. Soon after 0900, carrier *Junyo* joined in with a raid of eighteen Vals escorted by eleven Zeros.

Meanwhile the original wave of Nagumo's airmen had encountered the Americans heading in the opposite direction. They took no action against *Hornet*'s first strike but when they sighted the small *Enterprise* group, Lieutenant Hidaka led the nine Zeros from *Zuiho* out of the sun in an attack which resulted in four Wildcats and four Avengers being either shot down or forced to ditch. The leader of *Enterprise*'s torpedo-planes, Lieutenant-Commander Collett, was among those killed. Only three Zeros were lost though the others had to turn back short of ammunition. *Hornet*'s second group skirted the aerial battle and so was able to avoid combat.

The remaining Japanese pilots pressed on towards their targets. Kinkaid had put 23 Wildcats from *Enterprise* and fifteen Wildcats from *Hornet* in the air but this was a good deal less than the number that had defended the American carriers at the Eastern Solomons. As in that earlier battle moreover, the inexperienced fighter-director officer faced a radar-screen cluttered with friendly aircraft and there was yet again an abysmal lack of radio-discipline which rendered continuous control of the interceptors quite impossible.

As a result, it was not until 0857, when the attackers were only 45 miles away, that they were correctly identified on the radar-screen and even then hardly any of the Wildcats were able to engage them.

Enterprise had found refuge beneath a rain-squall at 0900, just before the Japanese appeared, so the full fury of the onslaught fell on *Hornet*. At 0910, fifteen Vals plunged down, while the Kate torpedo-planes hurtled in from astern, low over the water, in a perfectly co-ordinated assault.

Not even the tremendous AA fire put up by the carrier and her screening vessels could deter the Japanese airmen. A bomb hit the starboard side of *Hornet*'s flight deck aft. Two others scored very near misses. The Val flown by the squadron commander, Lieutenant-Commander Seki (who had also led the attack on *Enterprise* at the Eastern Solomons), was fatally hit, but, trailing a long column of flame, Seki deliberately dived into *Hornet*'s superstructure, wrecking her signal bridge; after which his aircraft crashed on through the flight deck, where two of its bombs exploded, starting a furious fire.

Before *Hornet*'s crew had had time to recover, two torpedoes struck her starboard side, flooding the forward engine-room and two boiler-rooms, severing electric cables, cutting off all power and communications. As the carrier slowed to a halt, amidst clouds of smoke and steam, three more bombs found their mark, one exploding on the flight deck but the others penetrating deep into the hull before detonating. Finally a blazing Kate torpedo-bomber, with a doomed pilot at the controls, came charging on to dash itself into the carrier's bow close by the forward elevator. It was all over in ten minutes.

The raiders paid heavily for their success. Of the fifteen Vals which had dived on *Hornet*, twelve fell to her anti-aircraft fire. About half the Kates had also been lost and their leader, Lieutenant Imajuku, was dead. Yet they left the carrier burning from bow to stern, totally immobilized, with 111 of her crew killed and 108 wounded.

As Nagumo's airmen turned away, their American counterparts were also preparing to attack, though without the same co-ordination. The Avengers in *Hornet*'s first wave, together with four of the escorting Wildcats, lost touch with their dive-bombers in cloud. Failing to find the enemy 'flat-tops', they launched their torpedoes at heavy cruiser *Suzuya* in Abe's Vanguard Group; however, she evaded these. The remnants of the *Enterprise* strike also attacked Abe's vessels, concentrating on battleship *Kirishima*, but again had no success.

Hornet's second wave also assaulted the Vanguard Group, with better fortune. The Avengers made a bomb attack on heavy cruiser

Tone which did no damage but at 0920, the Dauntless dive-bombers scored three hits and two very misses on heavy cruiser *Chikuma* which wounded Captain Komura, killed most of the personnel on the bridge, reduced her speed and compelled her to limp back to base.

By far the most effective raid, however, was that of the fifteen Dauntlesses in *Hornet's* first wave. These sighted Kondo's Advance Force at 0915. They were attacked by nine Zeros from *Junyo* but the four remaining Wildcats kept these away, though at the cost of two of their own number. The dive-bombers continued their search for carriers and at 0930 they were finally rewarded by the sight of *Shokaku* and *Zuiho*.* A swarm of twenty Zeros then engaged the Dauntlesses, shooting down one, the crew of which were killed, damaging two others so badly that they had to return to their carrier – one crashing on the way with the loss of its crew – and forcing the aircraft flown by the air group leader, Lieutenant-Commander Widhelm, to ditch. Widhelm and his gunner took to their life-raft, from which they had a splendid view of subsequent events. They were rescued by a Catalina two days later.

Command of the eleven remaining dive-bombers was taken over by Lieutenant Vose who, seeing that *Zuiho* was still burning, concentrated his entire force against *Shokaku*. Diving through anti-aircraft fire with Zeros still harassing them from above, the Dauntlesses hit Nagumo's flagship with four 1,000-pound bombs, wrecking her flight deck, her hangars and her elevators, reducing her speed to 21 knots, causing about 100 casualties and putting her out of action for nine vital months. Not one of Vose's aircraft was lost.

This might seem an effective retaliation for the crippling of *Hornet* but whereas the Americans had now struck their blows, the Japanese still had two formations airborne. Moreover the enemy, who had at first believed that *Hornet* was the only US carrier on hand, had learned from the chatter of the American pilots that *Enterprise* also was present. It was against her therefore that the next raids were directed.

Enterprise had now emerged from the rain-squall. She had hastily refuelled her Wildcats, 24 of which were on patrol overhead. At about 1000, radar on battleship *South Dakota* located the aircraft from *Shokaku* and *Zuikaku*, then about 55 miles away, but the carrier's

---

* *Zuikaku* was some distance to the east, under cover of a rain-squall.

radar did not give confirmation until the attackers had closed the range to 26 miles, and in any case the defending fighters were never directed to intercept them – perhaps because all attention had been diverted to a quite different danger.

Undetected by the Americans, submarine *I-21* had moved into position to attack *South Dakota*. Lieutenant Pollock, the pilot of one of the Wildcats, suddenly noticed the track of a torpedo racing towards destroyer *Porter* which was then picking up the crew of a ditched Dauntless. He dived down, firing his guns in a desperate attempt to detonate the torpedo or at least warn the destroyer. His only reward was to come under heavy, if fortunately inaccurate AA fire from her crew. They paid heavily for their ingratitude. At 1002, the torpedo tore into *Porter*'s boiler-room, crippling her and killing fifteen men.

None of the submarine's remaining torpedoes found a target but while the defenders were still in confusion, the Vals arrived overhead. At about 1015, without waiting for the torpedo-planes, their commander, Lieutenant Takahashi, led his men down to the assault.

They were met by a devastating volume of fire, especially from *Enterprise* and from *South Dakota*, manoeuvring close to the carrier. The battleship's skipper, Captain Thomas Gatch, was one of the US Navy's most controversial characters, who allowed his men to wear what they liked and his ship to become abominably dirty. His detractors claimed that discipline was lax and it must be admitted that *South Dakota* does seem to have been 'accident-prone'. In September, while on her way to the South Pacific, she had struck a coral pinnacle near Tongatabu, causing considerable damage. During the current battle, her communications system broke down and after it she was involved in a collision with destroyer *Mahan* while evading a suspected submarine. Yet, by incessant target practice, there is no doubt that Gatch had made his crew admirably proficient in the art of defending ships against air attack.

In consequence, dive-bomber after dive-bomber crashed into the sea all around Kinkaid's vessels. Although the Americans again exaggerated their achievements – *South Dakota* alone claimed to have downed considerably more Vals than took part in the raid – it seems that at least fifteen of the dive-bombers were in fact destroyed. Takahashi's own aircraft was badly damaged by a Wildcat. His rudder jammed, forcing him to fly in circles for about six hours before he ditched; he and his crew were later rescued by a Japanese tanker.

Nothing, however, could prevent two bombs from hitting *Enterprise*. One went through the flight deck, through the forecastle deck and out through the ship's side before exploding, but the second detonated near the forward elevator, which it put out of action. A very near miss, close to the starboard side aft, damaged a main turbine bearing and caused minor flooding. Of the carrier's crew, 44 were killed; 75 wounded.

Mercifully, *Enterprise* could still manoeuvre at speed. This proved her salvation when eleven dark-green Kates* appeared a short time later. Their leader, Lieutenant-Commander Murata, who had commanded the torpedo-bombers at Pearl Harbor, was shot down and killed by a Wildcat flown by Lieutenant Stanley Vejtasa but his pilots pressed on to launch torpedoes at *Enterprise* from both sides. Yet by skilful ship-handling Captain Hardison was able to avoid every one.

Destroyer *Smith* was less fortunate. A Kate, already badly damaged by the determined Lieutenant Vejtasa, did not drop its torpedo but instead deliberately flew with it into *Smith*'s forecastle, killing 28 men and injuring 23 others. The entire forward part of the destroyer turned into a mass of flames but these were eventually mastered by splendid damage control, aided by the unusual yet highly effective action of her skipper, Lieutenant-Commander Wood, who put his ship's bow close behind *South Dakota* so as to use her foaming wake against the fires.

As the surviving torpedo-bombers began their retirement, the Wildcats attacked in full strength – and annihilated them. Vejtasa alone was credited with having downed six (including the one that rammed *Smith*). Ensign Gordon, although out of ammunition, made such a determined mock-attack on a low-flying Kate that it crashed while trying to evade him.

At 1121, most of *Junyo*'s aircraft also attacked *Enterprise*. Their crews, however, were very raw – not of the same calibre as the veterans from *Shokaku* and *Zuikaku*. They achieved only one more near-miss which caused minor damage.

About six minutes later, the stragglers from this raid attacked, scoring hits on *South Dakota* and light cruiser *San Juan*. The battleship

* One had turned back with engine-trouble.

was struck on her forward turret, the armoured roof of which prevented serious damage, though flying fragments killed one man and wounded 49 more including Captain Gatch. *San Juan* in contrast was saved by her total lack of armour; the bomb passed right through her thin plates before exploding. Both vessels careered about out of control for a few minutes but no collisions resulted and the problems were soon rectified. Of the eighteen Vals that had left *Junyo,* only six returned; their leader, Lieutenant Yamaguchi, was among those lost.

Enterprise could now recover aircraft from both American carriers, which had returned from the strikes on Nagumo or Abe, desperately short of fuel; several indeed were forced to ditch, their crews being rescued by destroyers. Those which landed so crowded *Enterprise's* decks – the confusion being aggravated by her damaged elevator – that she was quite unable to provide fighter protection for *Hornet.* It was known that Kondo still possessed two undamaged carriers, as well as a much superior surface force. The torpedoing of *Porter* had shown that at least one submarine was in the vicinity. Despite later criticisms, Kinkaid really had no choice but to withdraw America's last remaining operational aircraft carrier from its present perilous position.

So at 1400, *Enterprise* retreated to the south-east. The luckless *Porter* was finished off by gunfire from destroyer *Shaw* after her crew had been taken off : 'sad but necessary' comments Morison 'with the enemy so near'.

There still seemed a slight hope of saving a more important cripple. By 1009, *Hornet's* crew, aided by hoses from destroyers *Morris* and *Russell* alongside, had got all fires under control. Heavy cruiser *Northampton* was preparing to take the carrier in tow. At this precise moment, a single Val – which had separated from its colleagues, then preparing to assault *Enterprise* – came hurtling down. Its bomb missed but operations were delayed as *Hornet's* escorts prepared to repulse further attacks.

None, however, were forthcoming, so by 1123, *Northampton* had taken the carrier in tow, only for the cable to break. A stronger one was attached by 1330, with which the heavy cruiser pulled the listing *Hornet* towards safety at a painful three knots. Meanwhile all but a handful of her crew were taken off by destroyers *Russell* and *Hughes;* this evacuation was completed by 1440.

Vice-Admiral Kondo, however, was determined that neither *Hornet* nor *Enterprise* should live to fight again. At about 1230, *Zuikaku* and *Junyo* reversed course to the south-east, while damaged *Shokaku* and *Zuiho* withdrew from the battle area. Kondo's own vessels and Abe's Vanguard Group had already set off towards the Americans about an hour earlier, hoping for a surface action after nightfall. And at 1315, nine Kates and five Zeros left *Junyo* to renew the attacks from the air.

Two hours later, the Japanese airmen sighted *Hornet*. *Northampton* hastily slipped the tow, gathering speed just in time to avoid the torpedoes aimed at her. Of the nine Kates, seven did not return to their carrier, their leader, Lieutenant Irikiin, was killed and only one torpedo found its mark – but they had done enough. *Hornet*'s starboard side was torn open. Water poured into her after engine-room, increasing her list to 14 degrees. Captain Mason ordered the remainder of her crew to abandon her.

Before they could do so, at 1540, six Vals and nine Zeros made their appearance but were driven off by gunfire. At 1555, a high-level bombing attack by six more aircraft scored a hit on her flight deck. Finally at 1702, by which time the carrier had already been abandoned, a formation of four Vals and six Zeros from *Junyo* made a final hit with a bomb that exploded in *Hornet*'s hangar.

Still *Hornet* would not sink. Her durability was now an embarrassment to the Americans, for Yamamoto had given orders to capture the carrier which he hoped could be towed to Truk as a spectacular demonstration of the Imperial Navy's success, and Rear-Admiral Abe, who had been kept informed of her plight by his reconnaissance floatplanes, was approaching rapidly with his formidable Vanguard Group.

Therefore, although the bulk of the American forces now retired, destroyers *Mustin* and *Anderson* were left to ensure that *Hornet* went down. Unfortunately the abysmal lack of reliability for which American torpedoes of the time were notorious, resulted in seven of the sixteen fired at the carrier failing to hit her. The other nine failed to sink her. *Mustin* and *Anderson* then poured 430 5-inch shells into her before, at about 2040, they were forced into hasty retreat as the Japanese closed in on them. However, since by then the wretched 'flat-top' was little more than a floating furnace, there was no question of Abe, when he reached the scene at about 2100, doing more than administering the *coup de grâce*.

Destroyers *Makigumo* and *Akigumo* were entrusted with this task. They had no problems with their torpedoes. Four 'Long Lances' finished *Hornet* – and the Battle of Santa Cruz.

CHAPTER SIX

The Battle of Guadalcanal

There can be no dispute that the Imperial Navy won the Battle of Santa Cruz. *Enterprise*, badly handicapped by her damaged elevator, was now the only American carrier in the South Pacific. So alarming did the situation appear, that the US Navy felt compelled to ask that a British carrier be sent to the combat area. As a result, HMS *Victorious* ultimately arrived at Pearl Harbor, though because of previous commitments, she did not do so until March 1943. She then had to re-equip with American aircraft so that she could replace any losses suffered, and train her ship's company and aircrews in American methods. A further two months therefore elapsed before she sailed to Noumea and by that time the period of crisis was over.

Vice-Admiral Kondo, however, showed little inclination to follow up his success. During the night of 26/27th October, his fleet was attacked by Catalinas, one of which narrowly failed to torpedo carrier *Zuikaku*, while another damaged destroyer *Terutsuki*, though not very seriously. The Japanese remained in the area in which the action had taken place until early on the following afternoon, when they began a general retirement to Truk.

Furthermore, although the battle had cost the Americans 74 aircraft, only 20 of these had fallen in combat, whereas 69 Japanese machines had been shot down and 23 more had ditched. About 140 of their crewmen had been killed, the majority irreplaceable veterans, including, as will have been noticed, virtually all their dive-bomber and torpedo-plane commanders. Such were the casualties that Kondo did not have sufficient aircrews remaining to man *Zuikaku* which was thereby in effect put out of action. Only *Hiyo* and *Junyo* would be available for the next major action and the declining standards of the Japanese pilots would become ever more apparent in the future.

On the other hand, for the moment at least the Japanese success at Santa Cruz – which they rather grandly entitled 'The Sea Battle of the South Pacific' – did serve to revive their morale; the more so since they greatly over-estimated their achievements. They determined to make one last massive effort to secure Guadalcanal by a 'systematic concentration of fighting forces'.

The bulk of the forces that were to be concentrated were the officers and men of Lieutenant-General Tadayoshi Sano's 38th ('Hiroshima') Division. Yamamoto planned to deliver the main body of the division in mid-November. In the meantime, a preliminary build-up of troops would be made by resuming the nightly missions of the 'Tokyo Express'.

The first of these was also the most futile. It will be remembered that after the failure of his attacks on Henderson Field, Maruyama had directed Colonel Shoji's men to make for Koli Point to the east of the American positions. On 2nd-3rd November, the 'Tokyo Express' provided Shoji with a small number of reinforcements but a large amount of equipment, ammunition and rations – so that he could march back round the American perimeter to re-join the main Japanese forces west of the Matanikau, where Hyakutake had now determined to muster the whole of his command.

Ironically, the Americans were much alarmed by this episode, which they believed indicated a planned 'pincer movement' on their perimeter from both flanks. Vandegrift, who had been warned about the Koli Point mission by Halsey, who in turn had been notified by the American code-breakers, therefore abandoned the somewhat ineffective operations which he had been conducting on his western flank in order to dispatch a strong body of Marines and soldiers to eliminate the danger from the east. The 'Cactus Air Force' also set out, looking for the Japanese ships, but since the night was pitch-black, the dive-bombers failed to find their targets and three of them crashed in a thunderstorm. Lieutenant-Commander Eldridge was among those who lost their lives.

Later air attacks were not very profitable either, for the pilots accidentally attacked their own ground-troops. Heavy cruiser *San Francisco*, light cruiser *Helena* and destroyer *Sterett* bombarded enemy positions to better effect but needlessly as Shoji was bent only on retreating. Leaving behind a small but determined rear-guard of about 450 men to fend off the Americans, he set off on his march. It was not until 12th November, that the last of the rear-guard were

killed or committed suicide having inflicted a casualty-list of 40 dead,
120 wounded on their opponents. By this time, Shoji's main body
was well on the way to safety. Subsequent American attacks inflicted
further losses but almost 2,000 Japanese troops made good their
escape.

Long before they could join him, however, Hyakutake had received
plenty of other reinforcements. On 5th November, a 'Tokyo Express'
reached Guadalcanal without opposition. Two days later, attacks by
seven Dauntlesses and three Avengers against a force of eleven destroyers caused considerable damage to *Takanami* and *Naganami* yet
did not prevent over 1,300 men coming ashore at Tassafaronga. On
the 8th, the PT-boats engaged another 'Tokyo Express', hitting but
not seriously harming destroyer *Mochitsuki*. On the 9th, Lieutenant-
General Sano, his staff, headquarters personnel and over 600 troops
were landed safely. On the 10th, five more destroyers defied a raid by
twelve dive-bombers to unload more men and supplies.

These new arrivals brought the Japanese soldiers on Guadalcanal
to 30,000, which for the first time gave them a superiority over Vandegrift's forces; yet the majority of them, having been on the island for
some time, were suffering from disease, wounds, or both. Large
numbers of fresh troops were needed before Hyakutake could drive
the Americans from their positions.

Vandegrift was receiving reinforcements of his own during this
period – as well as an encouraging visit from Halsey on 8th November. Even more encouraging was the arrival, on 30th October, of a
convoy (escorted by light cruiser *Atlanta* and destroyers *Aaron Ward*,
Benham, Fletcher and *Lardner*) bringing the M-2 'Long Tom' 155-mm
howitzers that Vandegrift so desperately needed to out-range Japan's
'Pistol Petes'. Destroyer *Lansdowne* reached the island on 7th November, with 90 tons of ammunition, and preparations were being made
to bring in more supplies as soon as shipping was available.

Also on 7th November, Geiger who badly needed a rest, was
succeeded by his former Chief of Staff, Louis Woods, now a Brigadier-
General. The new commander of 'Cactus Air Force' was not left short
of machines. Already on 29th October, Major Joseph Sailer, destined
to be Guadalcanal's most brilliant dive-bomber pilot, had flown in
with the Dauntlesses of Marine Squadron 132. A Wildcat unit,
Marine Squadron 112, arrived on 2nd November. On the 7th, Woods

The Battle of Santa Cruz: Attack on US Battleship *South Dakota*.

The Battle of Santa Cruz: Attack on US Light Cruiser *San Juan*.

American Commanders at the Naval Battle of Guadalcanal: (*Left to right*) Rear-Admiral Callaghan; Rear-Admiral Scott; Rear-Admiral Lee.

US Battleship *Washington*, flagship of Rear-Admiral Lee at the Naval Battle of Guadalcanal.

received twelve P-39 Airacobras and six Dauntlesses. On the 12th, ten dive-bombers, six Avengers and three Wildcats joined his command. Finally on the 13th, sixteen of the big, twin-engined, twin-fuselaged, twin-tailed P-38 Lockheed Lightnings reached Guadalcanal, to bring 'Cactus Air Force' for the first time to an operational strength of over 100 aeroplanes.

Though the Japanese could not prevent the American build-up from the air, they attempted to interrupt the seaborne supply route with their submarines. This was a move that could well have been attempted earlier, yet it had singularly little effect. *I-15* was sunk on 2nd November by destroyer *McCalla*; *I-172* on the 10th by minesweeper *Southard*.* In return *I-20* torpedoed cargo-ship *Majaba* on the 7th; she was forced to beach though she was later salvaged. The next successful attack on a transport, however, did not take place until the 28th, when a midget submarine, launched by *I-16*, torpedoed *Alchiba*, which also was beached but salvaged. By that time, in any event, the entire strategic situation had changed.

Yamamoto was now preparing to strike Japan's decisive blow. On the night of 12/13th November, Abe, now promoted to Vice-Admiral, would lead a bombardment unit including battleships *Hiei* and *Kirishima* to destroy Henderson Field. Then, next day, under the distant cover of Kondo's carriers, *Hiyo* and *Junyo*, Rear-Admiral Tanaka, who had resumed his earlier role after a temporary spell of duty escorting battleships, would carry the remaining 10,000 soldiers of the 38th Division, together with the 3,500 men of a specially organized Combined Naval Landing Force, to Guadalcanal. These reinforcements should be enough to enable Hyakutake to over-run Vandegrift's defences if only by sheer weight of numbers.

Fortunately for the Americans, their code-breakers were able to give adequate warning of Yamamoto's scheme, thus allowing them to take counter-measures. Kinkaid set out from Noumea on 11th November, with *Enterprise*, battleships *Washington* (flagship of Rear-Admiral Willis Lee) and *South Dakota*, heavy cruiser *Northampton*, light cruiser *San Diego* and eight destroyers. Repair parties were still working desperately on *Enterprise*'s crippled forward lift but it remained

* *I-22* was also lost, probably in late October, though the exact date is unknown, as is the cause of her disappearance; it may have been due to an accident, not to enemy action.

jammed and no one dared to lower it because if it had refused to be raised again, the carrier would have been useless. As it was, all aircraft had to be brought to or from her flight deck by the after elevator, which greatly restricted flying operations.

In addition, Rear-Admiral Turner had decided to provide Vandegrift with reinforcements before Tanaka could arrive. On 9th November, cargo-ships *Zeilin*, *Libra* and *Betelgeuse*, escorted by Rear-Admiral Scott in light cruiser *Atlanta* with destroyers *Aaron Ward*, *Fletcher*, *Lardner* and *McCalla*, left Espiritu Santo, carrying Marine replacements, ground personnel for 'Cactus Air Force', provisions and ammunition. A day earlier, Turner, with transports *McCawley*, *Crescent City*, *President Adams* and *President Jackson*, on which were embarked the officers and men of the 182nd Infantry Regiment, set out from Noumea. Heavy cruiser *Portland* and destroyers *Barton*, *Monssen*, *O'Bannon* and *Shaw* provided protection and en route to Guadalcanal the convoy was joined by Rear-Admiral Daniel Callaghan, commanding heavy cruisers *San Francisco* (flagship) and *Pensacola*, light cruisers *Helena* and *Juneau* and destroyers *Cushing*, *Laffey*, *Sterett*, *Gwin*, *Preston* and *Buchanan*.

Though the Americans had thus beaten the Japanese to Guadalcanal, their forces did not remain unchallenged. Submarine *I-31*, which carried a seaplane, had been sent to reconnoitre the approaches to the Solomons. On 10th November, her scout sighted and was sighted by Scott's convoy, so when these vessels reached Guadalcanal at daybreak on the 11th, they commenced unloading at top speed before the expected air attack could begin.

This was duly delivered by nine Vals from carrier *Hiyo*, then operating north of the Solomons. Engaged by Wildcats and heavy AA fire, the raiders damaged cargo-ship *Zeilin* by near-misses, but she disembarked all her troops and half her cargo before retiring to Espiritu Santo, escorted by destroyer *Lardner*. Five of the dive-bombers were shot down as were four escorting Zeros, though 'Cactus Air Force' lost six fighters and four pilots. Later in the day, 25 Bettys from Rabaul bombed Henderson Field at the cost of four of their number. Only one Wildcat fell, its pilot escaping unhurt.

Next day, Turner and Callaghan arrived. Again the troopships began to get their soldiers and supplies ashore with the minimum of delay. At 1317, Lieutenant Paul Mason, the same coastwatcher who, on 7th August, had notified Turner of the very first raid against American transports, sent warning of the approach of 21 Bettys armed with torpedoes, escorted by twelve Zeros. As on that earlier occasion, the American commander took his vessels to sea, screened by the warships and covered by a strong patrol of fighters, ready to meet the assault.

When the enemy aircraft were sighted at 1405 therefore, they encountered such determined opposition from American airmen and American anti-aircraft gunners that not a single torpedo found its mark. Four of the defending fighters were lost but hardly any Zeros and only a solitary Betty returned to their base. Two of the US warships suffered injuries but those to destroyer *Buchanan* were caused by 'friendly' AA fire. Heavy cruiser *San Francisco* was deliberately rammed by a crippled Betty which killed 24 men and wounded 45 more but caused only minor damage. The transports returned to their unloading area.

Turner, however, was still anxious. During the morning Abe's ships had been spotted by Flying Fortresses 335 miles to the north and the presence of *Hiei* and *Kirishima* was duly reported. By dusk, Turner had got all the American reinforcements, plus 90 per cent of their supplies, ashore, so felt well able to withdraw his vulnerable transports together with the two remaining cargo-vessels of Scott's group. Yet he did not dare to leave Abe free to eliminate Henderson Field. Kinkaid's battleships were still too far away to help, so all that Turner could do was instruct Callaghan to put up whatever defence was possible with his escorting warships.

These had now been reduced in number. On arrival in the Solomons, heavy cruiser *Pensacola* and destroyers *Preston* and *Gwin* – oddly it seems in retrospect – had been sent to reinforce Kinkaid. Destroyers *Shaw, McCalla* and damaged *Buchanan* were detached to escort the retiring transports. Even with the addition of Scott's remaining warships, Callaghan's Task Group 67:4 consisted only of two heavy cruisers, three light cruisers and eight destroyers.

Nor was Callaghan well qualified to fight the coming battle. Having served until recently as Ghormley's Chief of Staff, he had not had previous experience of a night-action. Perhaps it was for this reason that, like Crutchley before Savo Island, he neglected to issue to the ships which he commanded, either a battle plan or even a situation report based on his information about the enemy's movements.

As Scott had done at Cape Esperance, Callaghan formed his vessels into a single long column, with his cruisers in the middle and his destroyers divided between van and rear. This formation would, he hoped, facilitate communications, thus enabling him to retain a greater control over his forces.* However, it would mean that none of his ships would be scouting far enough ahead of his main body to give adequate warning, that his van destroyers would have little opportunity to make torpedo-attacks, and that his rear destroyers would be unable to support them even if they did.

To make matters worse, Callaghan, like many another senior officer, did not appreciate the tremendous advantage given by the SG surface search radar. He should have placed the vessels that possessed this in the van of his formation. Instead the first three destroyers in his column – *Cushing, Laffey* and *Sterett* – all lacked modern radar equipment. Destroyer *O'Bannon*, fourth in line, was the first ship with an SG set.

Behind the destroyers steamed Scott's flagship, light cruiser *Atlanta*, with only the older, inferior SC radar. Next came Callaghan's flagship. Although the course of events at Cape Esperance had shown that it was very important for the commanding officer to have the best possible radar under his own eye, Callaghan had chosen to fly his flag in heavy cruiser *San Francisco* which also carried only an SC set.†

The flagship was followed by heavy cruiser *Portland*; then by light cruiser *Helena* which did have SG radar; then by light cruiser *Juneau*. Behind the cruisers came destroyers *Aaron Ward, Barton* and *Monssen*. Stationed at the very end of the column was *Fletcher*, the only destroyer apart from *O'Bannon* with a superior radar installation. The Task Group moved slowly westward over the black waters of Iron-bottom Sound, through a dark, cloudy, moonless night, occasionally lit up by vivid flashes of lightning.

Meanwhile Abe's bombardment unit had entered the Slot between Santa Isabel and Florida. Captain Setoyama with destroyers *Shigure*,

* It has also been argued that it would assist navigation in the restricted waters around Savo Island, but it is worth remarking that the Japanese seem to have found no difficulty in adopting a formation in which their destroyers were thrown out ahead and on either flank of their battleships.

† Callaghan's choice of flagship may have been dictated, in part at least, by sentiment. He had been skipper of *San Francisco* from May 1941 to May 1942.

Shiratsuyu and *Yugure* was detached to guard the channel between the west coast of Guadalcanal and the Russell Islands. Abe's main body steered south-eastward so as to leave Savo Island to port. Battleships *Hiei* (flagship) and *Kirishima* were escorted by light cruiser *Nagara* (flagship of Rear-Admiral Susumu Kimura) and six destroyers, which were stationed in an arrowhead formation with the light cruiser at its point, destroyers *Yukikaze*, *Amatsukaze* and *Terutsuki* to port and *Akatsuki*, *Inadzuma* and *Ikazuchi* to starboard.

Unlike Callaghan, Abe had sent other destroyers well ahead of his main formation: *Yudachi* and *Harusame* to port; *Asagumo, Murasame* and *Samidare* to starboard. However, at about midnight, the Japanese entered a heavy rain-squall to the north-west of Savo. Abe reversed course temporarily until it had passed. During this manoeuvre the three advanced destroyers to starboard lost their proper station and fell back on the port quarter of the battleships.

Though his lookouts were as alert as ever, Abe did not anticipate that he would encounter anything bigger than a PT-boat, since Japanese reconnaissance aircraft which had observed the departure of Turner's transports, had reported, quite wrongly, that they had been accompanied by all their escorting warships. Accordingly the battleships' guns had been loaded with high-explosive bombardment shells rather than the armour-piercing type designed for use against ships. On the other hand, the Japanese had flashless cordite which would help to conceal their position in a night-action, whereas the Americans, who did not, would tend to be blinded by their own gunfire. And of course the Japanese as always had the outstanding advantage of their 'Long Lance' torpedoes.

Abe's vessels passed to the south of Savo Island at a speed of 23 knots. As they did so, they were detected by *Helena*'s radar. Captain Hoover, who had been the first to report enemy warships at Cape Esperance, was the first to report them again – on this occasion far more promptly. The time was 0124 on 13th October: Friday, the 'Bloody Thirteenth'.

*

Although they had thus been given a glorious opportunity to take their foes by surprise, it was the thirteen American ships that were to be the unlucky ones. Callaghan steered straight for the hostile

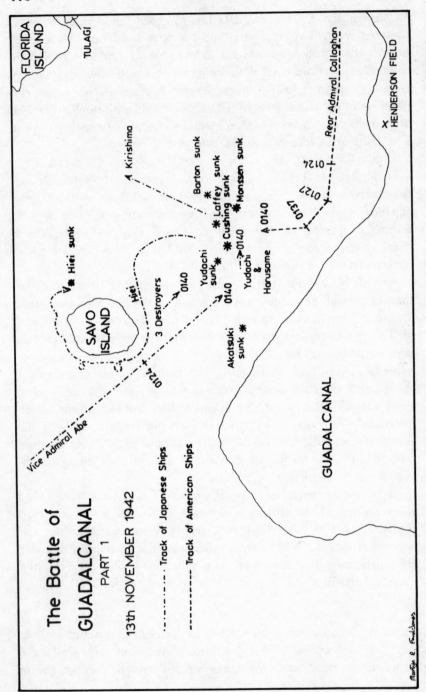

The Battle of
GUADALCANAL
PART 1

13th NOVEMBER 1942

—·—·— Track of Japanese Ships

— — — Track of American Ships

FLORIDA ISLAND

TULAGI

SAVO ISLAND

GUADALCANAL

HENDERSON FIELD

Kirishima

Hiei sunk

Hiei

3 Destroyers

0140

Yudachi sunk

0140

Akatsuki sunk

Barton sunk

Laffey sunk

Cushing sunk

Monssen sunk

0140

Yudachi & Harusame

0140

0137

0127

0124

Rear Admiral Callaghan

0124

Vice Admiral Abe

formation, calling over the TBS to *Helena* and *O'Bannon* for further information on its progress. Again their bad radio discipline greatly handicapped the Americans. All their ships spoke at the same time, the bedlam of orders, acknowledgements and requests causing total confusion. Perhaps this was the reason why it was not until 0137 that Callaghan ordered a change of course to due north and an increase of speed to 20 knots. By this manoeuvre he hoped to 'cross the enemy's T' as Scott had done at Cape Esperance. Unfortunately, he had left it too late.

Only four minutes later, destroyer *Cushing* at the head of the American column suddenly sighted *Yudachi* and *Harusame* crossing her bow from port to starboard at a range of 3,000 yards. Lieutenant-Commander Parker hastily turned to port to avoid collision and get into a position from which he could launch torpedoes. As the other American vessels followed him round, their formation became badly disorganized. *Cushing* called for permission to fire torpedoes but by the time Callaghan gave this, *Yudachi* and *Harusame* had vanished into the darkness. Other Japanese ships were soon in sight, however, for *Cushing*'s action had taken the American column right into the centre of the enemy force.

Meanwhile Abe had been warned by his scouting destroyers of their encounter with *Cushing*. His battleships therefore had precious time in which to change the ammunition immediately available from bombardment to armour-piercing shells. Furthermore although at 0145, Callaghan had signalled 'Stand by to Open Fire', he did not give the command to do so because his formation was in such disarray that he feared his vessels might engage each other.

So it was the Japanese who struck first. At 0150, a searchlight from *Akatsuki* settled on the bridge of *Atlanta*. She promptly opened fire on the vessel illuminating her but in return both Japanese battleships as well as several destroyers turned their guns on her. A storm of shells fell on the light cruiser, one of them killing Rear-Admiral Scott and every other officer on the bridge except one. At the same moment, Callaghan at last gave the order: 'Odd ships commence fire to starboard; even ships to port'.*

---

* This order caused more confusion since not every American vessel could locate targets on the side designated. *Atlanta* for instance, though an odd-numbered ship, was already firing to port as she engaged *Akatsuki*.

Now most of the US warships joined in the action, which became a mad mêlée at point-blank range. A large number of the American shells were directed at *Akatsuki*, for her searchlight, though proving fatal to *Atlanta*, had also given away her own position. *Helena* and *O'Bannon* certainly fired on her, as did *Fletcher* at the rear of the column, though her skipper, Commander Cole, soon turned his attention elsewhere on observing that several of his colleagues had selected the same target. Sufficient projectiles found their mark to sink *Akatsuki* – first Japanese casualty of the three nights and two days of action that together would be known as the Naval Battle of Guadalcanal.

However, the Japanese were firing equally effectively and were not restricting themselves to the use of shells. One, possibly two, torpedoes struck the hapless *Atlanta*, bringing her to a shuddering halt, totally disabled.

Destroyer *Cushing* was damaged by gunfire from the enemy screening vessels which severed all power lines and reduced her speed. Despite this, she launched six torpedoes at *Hiei* but all missed. Then a searchlight from the battleship illuminated *Cushing* which was hit repeatedly and set on fire.

Laffey, directly astern of *Cushing*, also sent torpedoes at *Hiei*, but so close was she that there was not enough time for the warhead pistols to be activated, so her 'fish' bounced back harmlessly from the battleship's hull. *Laffey*'s machine-gunners riddled *Hiei*'s bridge, killing her skipper, Captain Suzuki. He did not remain unavenged for long. As *Laffey* pulled away, two 14-inch salvoes reduced her to a wreck. A destroyer then blew her stern off with a 'Long Lance'. She was hastily abandoned, to sink shortly afterwards.

Sterett, third in line, engaged enemy destroyers, which retaliated effectively with hits on her foremast and on her port side aft which disabled her steering gear. *Sterett* next fired four torpedoes at *Hiei*, all of which missed, then turned her 5-inch guns on the battleship, as also did *O'Bannon*.

San Francisco first fired at Japanese destroyers. After seven salvoes, however, she directed her attention towards 'a small cruiser or large destroyer' ahead of her at close range. The flagship put two full 8-inch salvoes into this vessel. Almost every shell hit the target, setting it ablaze from end to end. *San Francisco* next sent several well-placed salvoes into *Hiei*, as did the cruisers astern of her. *Kirishima* in contrast received only one 8-inch hit during the entire action; she continued to fire 'as if on manoeuvres'.

Shaken by the fury of the attack on his flagship, uncertain as to the size or strength of the force opposed to him, Abe ordered his battleships to turn to port, prior to withdrawing. It seemed that Callaghan had got the better of the encounter. However, at about 0155, he suddenly realized that the 'small cruiser or large destroyer' that he had previously devastated was in fact the wretched *Atlanta*. Horrified, he called out over the TBS : 'Cease Fire – Own Ships'.

It was a fatal mistake. As Captain DuBose of *Portland* queried this incomprehensible order, *San Francisco*, her own guns now silent, was illuminated by a Japanese searchlight. A full salvo from *Kirishima* crashed into her superstructure. On her shattered bridge, Rear-Admiral Callaghan, Captain Cassin Young and almost every member of Callaghan's staff fell dead or dying. Other hits reduced *San Francisco*'s speed and damaged her steering, putting her temporarily out of control.

The few American vessels that had taken any notice of Callaghan's command promptly resumed firing. Destroyer *Aaron Ward* attacked a target on the starboard bow, which she thought blew up. Of the Japanese scouts, *Harusame* had wisely pulled away to the north but *Yudachi* had re-entered the fight. She did approach the starboard flank of the American column and since, apart from *Akatsuki*, she was the only enemy destroyer to suffer serious harm, it seems probable that she was *Aaron Ward*'s victim – though the report that she had exploded was much exaggerated.

Most of the American warships, however, concentrated on *Hiei*, employing torpedoes as well as gunfire. *O'Bannon* aimed two 'fish' at Abe's flagship but without result. So close was the range that *Hiei* could not depress her 14-inch guns sufficiently; her shells passed over the destroyer. *Barton* launched four torpedoes. *Monssen* launched ten. Unfortunately the American weapons did not belie their poor reputation.

Even more regrettable was the fact that a number of 'Long Lances' were now racing towards the American formation and they maintained their high standard of effectiveness. One of them blew off most of *Portland*'s stern, including two of her propellers. Her damaged plates formed an unwanted rudder, which forced her to turn in circles.

Another 'Long Lance' ripped open *Juneau*'s forward engine-room, bringing her to a halt, flooding badly and out of action. Two more struck destroyer *Barton*, literally tearing her in half. She sank within seconds, taking down with her all but a handful of her crew.

Destroyer *Monssen* suffered a different but equally horrible catastrophe. Lieutenant-Commander McCombs, believing that star-shell illuminating his ship came from other American vessels, switched on his fighting lights. This merely gave the Japanese a clearly identifiable target. Hit by 37 shells, *Monssen* was reduced to a blazing hulk. Her crew could only take to their life-rafts. In the confusion, eight wounded men were left aboard but luckily they were rescued at daybreak. There was no question, however, of saving the destroyer. She finally blew up at about noon on 13th November. Having witnessed the fates of *Barton* and *Monssen*, Commander Cole wisely decided to withdraw *Fletcher* temporarily from the scene of combat.

At about this time also, *Portland*, while still out of control, sighted *Hiei*, then some 4,000 yards away, and turned her 8-inch guns onto the Japanese battleship. Almost every other undamaged American ship joined in. At such close range *Hiei* suffered severely. Over 50 shell-hits reduced her speed, damaged her steering and communications system and caused numerous fires in her superstructure. By 0200, she was retiring northward. *Kirishima*, although virtually untouched, also withdrew.

The destroyers on each side continued to exchange fire. *Cushing*, already badly damaged, received further hits. Her fires, which were just coming under control, broke out with still greater violence. At 0315, her crew were forced to abandon her, though she did not finally sink until late next afternoon. *Aaron Ward* was also struck by at least nine shells; her injuries included a flooded engine-room which left her dead in the water.

Sterett proved more successful. Encountering the already damaged *Yudachi*, she fired two torpedoes, one at least of which hit its mark, bringing the Japanese destroyer to a halt. *Sterett* then directed her guns onto her opponent, causing such damage that the burning *Yudachi* had to be abandoned, her crew being rescued by destroyer *Samidare*. Shortly afterwards, however, *Sterett* was also hit, set on fire and forced out of the action. *Fletcher*, returning for a new attack, fired torpedoes – ten of them – but none found a target.

The firing died away soon after 0220. The Japanese had lost *Akatsuki* sunk and *Yudachi* abandoned. When dawn came, *Portland*, still circling out of control, fired six salvoes at *Yudachi*, the last of which struck home, causing her to explode and disappear. Destroyers *Ikazuchi*, *Murasame* and *Amatsukaze* had suffered trivial damage. The most serious casualty had been *Hiei* which was limping away slowly north of Savo, accompanied by destroyer *Yukikaze*. The battleship, still full of fight, shelled crippled *Aaron Ward* from a range of about thirteen miles but scored only near-misses.

On the American side, four destroyers had already gone down or been abandoned. The shattered *Atlanta* was taken in tow by tug *Bobolink* but she was clearly doomed and shortly after dark on the evening of the 13th, she had to be finished off by scuttling charges. The tug then transferred her help to *Portland* which finally limped into Tulagi Harbor, where she could carry out repairs, early on 14th November; as also did *Aaron Ward*.

Captain Hoover of *Helena*, now the senior officer, led the remaining vessels of Task Group 67:4 towards the safety of Espiritu Santo. *San Francisco*, *Juneau* and *Sterett* were all badly injured. Only *Helena*, *O'Bannon* and *Fletcher* were fully fit for action.* And the Americans' ordeal was not yet over. At about 1100, submarine *I-26* – the boat that had crippled carrier *Saratoga* – launched a salvo of torpedoes at *San Francisco*. They missed but one of them continued onwards, heading straight for *Juneau*. The damage to *San Francisco*'s communication system was so great that no warning could be given. Struck on her port side under the bridge, *Juneau* simply disintegrated with a colossal thunderclap, leaving only a vast cloud of smoke and, astonishingly, some 100 of her crew of about 700 clinging to the debris in the water.

Hoover was now faced with a ghastly decision. If he attempted rescue operations, he risked another torpedo attack with the strong possibility of losing a further ship or ships. He therefore signalled news of the sinking to a passing Flying Fortress, requesting that the information be forwarded to Halsey's headquarters; then he left the danger-zone as speedily as possible.

Unfortunately the bomber's message never reached Halsey. By the

---

* It is interesting that the only ships which escaped almost unscathed from the holocaust were those fitted with SG radar sets.

time that Catalinas reached the scene, all but ten of *Juneau*'s crew had died from wounds, thirst or attacks by blood-maddened sharks. Mr and Mrs Thomas Sullivan of Waterloo, Iowa, lost five sons – a tragedy within a tragedy which resulted in the issue of regulations forbidding relatives from serving in the same ship. It was perhaps the United States Navy's most miserable moment in the Guadalcanal campaign.

*

One of Vice-Admiral Halsey's least attractive traits was his unforgiving attitude towards subordinate commanders who were defeated by the despised Japanese. Halsey's endorsements on their action reports tended to show 'extreme displeasure' or be 'scathing indictments' – in contrast with the milder reactions of Nimitz. It is believed for instance that Callaghan, had he survived, might have been court-martialled for his errors. As it happened, it was the luckless Hoover who paid for the Americans' misfortunes, being deprived of his command for having abandoned *Juneau*'s survivors. Later, Halsey admitted that this was 'a grievous mistake' and that Hoover had acted for the best.

Other American officers vented their wrath against the enemy. *Kirishima* had retreated to safety but *Hiei* – which had now been joined by destroyers *Shigure, Shiratsuyu* and *Yugure* – was still north of Savo.* At 0615, five dive-bombers from Henderson Field attacked her, scoring a hit. Then, in the course of the next four hours, the 'Cactus Air Force' mounted three more assaults with bombs or torpedoes, though without achieving further results.

Meanwhile Rear-Admiral Kinkaid had launched nine Avengers and six Wildcats from *Enterprise* with orders to engage any targets encountered, then report to Vandegrift. At about 1020, they broke through low clouds to deliver simultaneous torpedo attacks on *Hiei* from both bows. The battleship fired a 14-inch salvo at them but in vain. Two torpedoes struck her, rendering her unmanoeuvrable.

Relentlessly the American airmen continued to strike at *Hiei*. Fourteen Flying Fortresses dropped 56 500-pound bombs but these merely covered her with clouds of spray. Yet another attack by six

---

* *Hiei*'s distress signals were intercepted by American code-breakers who, it has been reported, notified Vandegrift's airmen of her position. Since, however, dawn had found her within plain view of American warships, it seems unlikely that such information was necessary.

torpedo-planes from Henderson Field did no damage but an assault by six Dauntlesses scored three bomb-hits. The decisive raid was made at about 1430, by *Enterprise*'s Avengers, now operating from Guadalcanal. Of the four torpedoes which found their mark, two bounced off the battleship's hull without exploding, but the others left her dead in the water. By 1800, *Hiei*'s crew had been taken off by her screening destroyers. She sank about an hour later, carrying 450 officers and men down with her. Abe was dismissed from his command by Yamamoto and left the Imperial Navy in the following March.

Hiei's loss did not cause the Japanese to abandon their plans. Tanaka's transports retired temporarily but made preparations to advance down the Slot next day; while early on 13th November, Vice-Admiral Mikawa sailed from Shortland Island to carry out the bombardment that Abe had failed to execute. Unlike Abe, he would meet with no surface opposition, apart from gallant but unsuccessful attacks by a pair of PT-boats. Halsey had detached Lee's battleships from *Enterprise*'s escorts with orders to proceed to Ironbottom Sound but the carrier's slow progress, caused by her need to steam into the wind when launching or landing her aircraft, had resulted in Lee being too far away to reach Guadalcanal in time.

Mikawa arrived off Savo Island soon after midnight. He remained on patrol in this area with heavy cruisers *Chokai* (flagship) and *Kinugasa*, light cruiser *Isuzu* and a pair of destroyers, while Rear-Admiral Shoji Nishimura with his flagship, heavy cruiser *Suzuya*, another heavy cruiser, *Maya*, light cruiser *Tenryu* and six more destroyers, closed in to deliver the bombardment by the light of flares dropped from scouting float-planes. At 0205 on 14th November, Nishimura's vessels withdrew after firing almost 1,000 shells. One dive-bomber and seventeen fighters had been wrecked, several other aircraft had been damaged, but Henderson Field was still operational. Had Abe's battleships shelled the air-strip, it would probably have been a different story.

With daylight, American air-power was again in the ascendancy. At 0730, scouts from Henderson Field spotted Tanaka's Reinforcement Group – eleven transports escorted by eleven destroyers and covered by Zeros from *Hiyo* and *Junyo* – steaming down the Slot. This sighting marked the beginning of a terrible day for the Japanese convoy, but for a time at least its fate was postponed as 'Cactus Air

Force' sought revenge against Mikawa's bombardment unit.

At about 0800, these vessels were attacked by six Avengers, seven Dauntlesses and seven Wildcats from Guadalcanal. The dive-bombers hit heavy cruiser *Maya* but as usual torpedoes did the gravest harm, two of them badly damaging heavy cruiser *Kinugasa.*

Then Kinkaid's airmen took a hand. Two of his pilots, Lieutenant Gibson and Ensign Buchanan, had discovered Mikawa's force at about 0750. After reporting their sighting, they trailed the enemy for well over an hour until, at 0915, with fuel running low, they dived to the attack, both hitting the injured *Kinugasa* with 500-pound bombs.

By this time, seventeen dive-bombers and ten fighters from *Enterprise* were well on their way towards the target. They arrived at about 1015. A very near miss apparently finished off *Kinugasa*, which sank soon afterwards. Heavy cruiser *Chokai*, light cruiser *Isuzu* and destroyer *Michishio* were damaged, though all returned to Shortland Island. The airmen landed safely at Henderson Field.

Thereafter the Americans concentrated their attention on Tanaka. At 0830, two dive-bombers from *Enterprise* had attacked the convoy, one of them being shot down by the escorting Zeros. This, however, was the last success the Japanese fighters enjoyed for some time and despite suffering serious losses throughout the day, they utterly failed to protect their charges. The first major assault was made at about 1150, by seven torpedo-planes, eighteen dive-bombers and twelve fighters from Henderson Field. Transport *Sado Maru*, crippled by bombs, had to return to Shortland Island, accompanied by two destroyers. Transports *Canberra Maru* and *Nagara Maru,* struck by both bombs and torpedoes, were sunk.*

It must now have been unpleasantly obvious to Tanaka that he would have to face a whole series of strikes from Henderson Field. Yet with his usual stubborn resolution, he continued his advance, transferring the troops from the sunken transports to his destroyers. At 1245, thirteen dive-bombers, plus an appropriate fighter escort, appeared. Transport *Brisbane Maru* was hit, broke in half and sank. Ten more dive-bombers attacked at about 1400.

---

* The word *maru*, included in the names of Japanese merchant vessels, had once been added to the names of aristocrats' sons during Japan's feudal age. To give it to a ship implies a personality, much in the same way that Europeans or Americans call a vessel 'she', not 'it'.

Half-an-hour later, Flying Fortresses from Espiritu Santo made high altitude bombing runs, the wobbling fall of their weapons leaving an indelible impression on Tanaka's mind, though as usual they had little effect on Japanese shipping. Far more dangerous was the raid by eight Dauntlesses and twelve Wildcats from *Enterprise* at about 1530. These sank *Shinanogawa Maru* and *Arizona Maru*, then flew to Henderson Field.

Kinkaid now had only eighteen fighters left aboard *Enterprise*. He therefore headed south and next day retired to Noumea. Vandegrift's airmen, however, remained in action, helped by the presence of many of the carrier's pilots. Shortly before dusk, nine dive-bombers and four torpedo-planes sank transport *Nako Maru*. Lieutenant-Colonel Bauer, the Guadalcanal fighter commander, who was leading the seven escorting Wildcats, was attacked by a Zero and forced to ditch. Rescue flights – which could not be sent out until after dark – failed to find him. Sometime that night, as Miller reports in *The Cactus Air Force* : 'Bauer died a lonely death swimming through a black sea, lit fitfully by the fires and the flickering shadows on the clouds. Perhaps it was a wound, perhaps exhaustion, perhaps a shark.' It was a fate faced by so many brave men on both sides during the course of the Guadalcanal campaign.

One final raid was made by seven unescorted dive-bombers. The absence of protecting fighters gave the Zeros their chance. They broke up the attack, downing three of the Dauntlesses and damaging all but one of the others. Darkness found the indomitable Tanaka still heading towards Guadalcanal with his last four transports.

Darkness also meant that the 'Cactus Air Force' could no longer defend the island. That duty now devolved upon Rear-Admiral Willis Lee. In the early evening of 14th November, his Task Force 64 – consisting of battleships *Washington* (flagship) and *South Dakota* and destroyers *Walke*, *Benham*, *Preston* and *Gwin* – was to be found to the north-west of Guadalcanal, steering for Ironbottom Sound.

Lee was a cool, quiet, thoughtful, immensely efficient officer, who was one of the few senior commanders with a detailed knowledge of the advantages and limitations of radar. Having been director of fleet training just before the war, he was probably not very happy that the vessels under his control were two battleships which had not previously operated together and four destroyers from four different divisions which had been assigned to him simply because they happened to be the ones which had the most fuel when Task Force 64 was detached from *Enterprise*'s screen. No doubt it was for this reason that, like Scott and Callaghan, he formed a single line ahead, with his destroyers leading the battleships.

Halsey had signalled to Lee that his objectives were the enemy transports 'plus targets encountered'. Task Force 64 would certainly meet more than transports for since 1000 that morning, a Japanese squadron under Vice-Admiral Kondo had been steaming south, determined to deliver a really effective blow against Henderson Field. Kondo had left battleships *Kongo* and *Haruna* and heavy cruiser *Tone* with *Hiyo* and *Junyo* but he took over some of the survivors of Abe's unit to form a striking force which must have seemed entirely adequate for such a mission.

Under his immediate control, Kondo had battleship *Kirishima*, heavy cruiser *Atago* (his flagship), heavy cruiser *Takao*, light cruiser *Nagara* (flagship of Rear-Admiral Kimura) and destroyers *Terutsuki*, *Hatsuyuki*, *Shirayuki*, *Inadzuma*, *Asagumo* and *Samidare*. Ahead was stationed an advance screen under Rear-Admiral Shintaro Hashimoto in light cruiser *Sendai*, accompanied by destroyers *Uranami*, *Ayanami* and *Shikinami*. During the afternoon, Kondo was attacked by US submarine *Trout*. Her torpedoes did no damage but she was able to report her encounter, thereby giving a vital warning to Lee.

That officer entered Ironbottom Sound at 2215. The offshore breeze brought with it a sweet scent of honeysuckle, in pleasant contrast to the stench of decay that usually drifted from Guadalcanal. It seemed a good omen. Less satisfactory was Vandegrift's inability to give Lee any further information as to the progress of the enemy.*

Although Lee was unaware of it, the Japanese advance screen, its presence concealed on his radar sets by the nearby land, was in fact following him at a distance of about seven miles. At 2210, the keen-eyed lookouts on *Sendai* had seen Task Force 64 silhouetted against the moonlight, though they reported the battleships only as 'cruisers'.

---

* Lee had not been given a voice-radio call sign, with the result that he experienced some difficulty in convincing Guadalcanal of his identity. He finally did so by using the nickname of 'Ching' Lee, by which he had been known to Vandegrift during his Naval Academy days.

Warning Kondo of the danger, Hashimoto detached destroyers *Uranami* and *Ayanami* to circle Savo to the west and south, while he continued to trail the Americans with his flagship and his remaining destroyer, *Shikinami*. Kondo also divided his formation. *Kirishima, Atago, Takao* and destroyers *Terutsuki* and *Asagumo* maintained their course, but Rear-Admiral Kimura with *Nagara* and the other four destroyers was sent ahead in support of *Uranami* and *Ayanami*. This multiple dispersion of the Japanese forces has been roundly criticized, yet it brought them very close to a spectacular success.

At 2252, Lee altered course to the west, intending to pass south of Savo. No sooner had he completed his turn than he at last detected the enemy on his radar. Shortly thereafter at 2312, *Sendai* and *Shikinami* were sighted by lookouts on both American battleships. Fire was opened at 2317, whereupon Hashimoto hastily retired under a smoke-screen.

Five minutes later, destroyer *Walke* at the head of Lee's column opened fire on *Uranami* and *Ayanami* which were then re-entering Ironbottom Sound after rounding Savo. *Benham* and *Preston* joined in but *Gwin*, sighting Kimura's vessels following the first two destroyers, engaged these new arrivals. The American battleships also fired with their secondary armament but *Washington*'s radar was hampered by the proximity of her targets to Savo, and at 2333, *South Dakota* suffered another of those mishaps that befell her all too often – this time an electric power failure which put her radar and hence her guns temporarily out of action. To add to the confusion, *Sendai* and *Shikinami* now came in to attack from astern.

As in previous night actions, the Japanese showed much the greater skill. *Ayanami* was badly damaged by the American destroyers, being left crippled south-east of Savo, but far more harm befell her opponents. *Walke*, hit several times, reeled out of the line. *Gwin* was struck in an engine-room, while another hit on her upper deck aft disrupted the safety links of her torpedoes, which slipped harmlessly overboard. *Preston* turned her attention to *Nagara* but in return shells from the light cruiser knocked down her after stack and exploded in her boiler-rooms, bringing her to a halt. Several enemy ships then poured a concentrated fire upon *Preston*. She had to be abandoned at 2336, sinking soon afterwards.

The US destroyers had neglected to fire torpedoes at what they

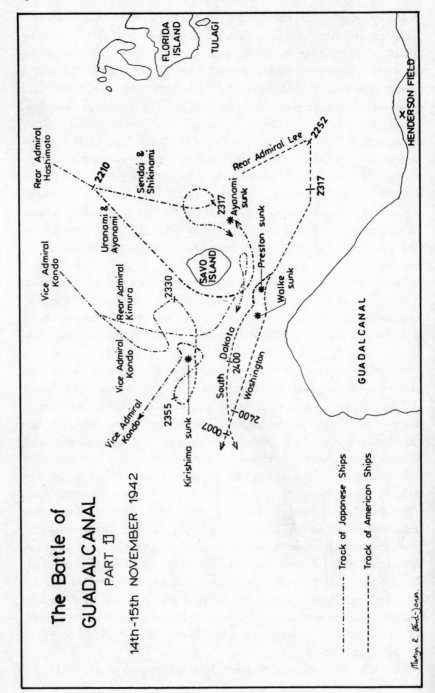

The Battle of
GUADALCANAL
PART II

14th–15th NOVEMBER 1942

Track of Japanese Ships
Track of American Ships

Merlyn R. (Bod.) Jones.

considered minor targets but the Japanese had no such inhibitions.* At 2338, the 'Long Lances' arrived. One shattered the bow of *Benham*, which turned away, out of the fight. Another blew off *Walke's* forecastle as far aft as the bridge, leaving her a blazing wreck. She sank four minutes later, whereupon her depth-charges, which had been reported as having been made 'safe', exploded immediately under her survivors.

Lee's battleships hastily turned to avoid the stricken destroyers – *Washington* to port; *South Dakota* to starboard. The latter, still handicapped by her radar failure lost contact with the flagship. She then encountered Kimura's vessels, which, at 2355, sent a warning to Kondo, before reversing course, releasing as they did so a swarm of 34 'Long Lances'. Incredibly, none of these found their mark.

On hearing of *South Dakota's* presence, Kondo, who had been keeping his heavy ships clear of the mêlée with the intention of delivering his bombardment once all opposition had been overcome, confidently, if rashly, headed towards her. Minutes after she had escaped Kimura's torpedoes, *South Dakota* was illuminated by Kondo's searchlights. Shells from 14-inch and 8-inch guns smashed into her, while destroyer *Asagumo* fired more torpedoes though fortunately these also missed. The American battleship, able to reply only by aiming at the searchlights, was in dire peril.

Yet, with dramatic suddenness, there came salvation. *Washington*, having drawn clear of the fighting, had obtained a clear picture on her radar. The biggest enemy target had been tracked for some time and at midnight, Lee opened fire with devastating effect at a range of 8,400 yards. Within seven minutes, nine hits by 16-inch shells, plus about 40 hits from *Washington's* 5-inch secondary armament, reduced *Kirishima* to a hulk, her superstructure in flames, two of her turrets destroyed, her steering gear wrecked.

South Dakota took advantage of what must have seemed a miraculous intervention to retire to the west, followed by *Benham* and *Gwin*. To draw attention from them as well as to intercept any more Japanese ships that might be approaching, Lee steered north-west. Kondo at first moved to follow, but at 0025, he thought better of it, abandoned

---

* The reason for this undoubtedly was that, unlike their foes, the Japanese could re-load their torpedo tubes in a matter of minutes; a capability at that time not only unknown to but unsuspected by the Americans.

his proposed bombardment and took his remaining vessels away under a smoke-screen.

Lee turned back at 0033. His manoeuvre was well timed for Tanaka, whose transports were now nearing Guadalcanal, had sent forward destroyers *Kagero* and *Oyashio* to attack any American warships encountered. These sighted *Washington* and promptly launched their torpedoes at her. Had she not changed course at the critical moment, they must have struck her; as it was, several exploded in her wake.

The Americans had paid a high price for having thwarted Kondo. *Walke* and *Preston* were already at the bottom of the sea. *South Dakota*, hit by 42 shells, with a turret out of action, her superstructure badly damaged, 38 men dead and 60 wounded, returned to the United States for repairs. *Benham*, limping away to Espiritu Santo, had to be abandoned at 1724 on 15th November, her crew being rescued by *Gwin*, which then finished her off by gunfire.

However, the crippling of *Kirishima* more than matched the American losses. Though her crew, aided by *Sendai* and four destroyers, tried to effect repairs, it was obvious that she would never be able to draw away from the island in time to escape the air-attacks from Henderson Field which would undoubtedly follow. The fate of *Hiei* must have haunted all memories.* It was decided that there was no point in submitting the wounded 'battlewagon' to a similar ordeal. Her survivors were transferred, sea valves were opened and at 0320 on 15th November, *Kirishima* disappeared beneath the waves northwest of Savo Island. Destroyer *Ayanami* was also scuttled after her crew had been taken off.

Kondo's inability to neutralize the airfield provided a further grim warning for Tanaka. In an attempt to get as many men and supplies as possible ashore, he radioed to Mikawa requesting permission to run his remaining four transports onto the beach at Tassafaronga. Mikawa refused but Kondo overruled him and by 0400, *Yamatsuki Maru*, *Kinugawa Maru*, *Hirokawa Maru* and *Yamaura Maru* were all hard aground. There was no time for Tanaka's destroyers to disembark the troops aboard them. They retired at high speed, were far enough away

---

* The American code-breakers, who intercepted *Kirishima*'s calls for help, reported that they were 'practically a replay' of the ones previously sent out by *Hiei*.

to escape the attention of the American airmen at daybreak, and ultimately got back safely to Shortland Island.

So the last phase of the action consisted of incessant attacks on the stranded transports, their crews, their passengers and the men trying to unload them. Miller in *The Cactus Air Force* lists seven separate air-raids. In between them, American artillery-pieces added to the destruction. Destroyer *Meade*, which had just escorted an auxiliary and a tug to Tulagi, joined in the attack from the sea; then rescued 135 survivors from *Walke* and 131 from *Preston* who had been watching proceedings from their life-rafts with pardonable approval.

By early afternoon it was all over – the transports gutted wrecks; their crews slaughtered. All the efforts of the Japanese, all their tenacity, all their sacrifices, had resulted in the arrival at Guadalcanal of only 2,000 demoralized soldiers, 260 cases of ammunition and 1,500 bags of rice. The Americans had won the most important battle : the battle of supplies.

CHAPTER SEVEN

The Battle of Tassafaronga

The victors followed up their victory. Food, equipment, medical supplies were shipped to Vandegrift's weary but undaunted troops. On Thursday 26th November, which was Thanksgiving Day – the American equivalent of Harvest Festival – the traditional meal of turkey and cranberry sauce was provided for all hands. By the end of the month, the number of PT-boats at Tulagi had increased to fifteen, while 124 aircraft, including eight Flying Fortresses and five New Zealand Hudsons, were based at Henderson Field or the two fighter strips.

However, when Vandegrift attempted to add success on land to that gained at sea, he found Japanese resistance as dogged as ever. On 18th November, he directed a series of thrusts against the enemy but all of them were checked. By the 23rd, the operations had to be suspended after making virtually no progress.

The Japanese indeed had not given up hope of winning back Guadalcanal. Yamamoto wanted to abandon the island, but Prime Minister Tojo, having transferred his principal objective in the South Pacific from New Guinea to Guadalcanal, obstinately refused to agree. He even ordered – far too late – that the Army Air Force should henceforth take part in actions over the Solomons.

Nonetheless, the Japanese realized that they could not prepare another major offensive for at least two months; 15th January 1943 was the date suggested. In the meantime, Yamamoto, following the loss of *Hiei* and *Kirishima*, had given up all intention of delivering future bombardments of Henderson Field; his heavy units were withdrawn to Truk, whence he hoped they might still be able to sortie for a decisive fleet action. Moreover the Japanese could no longer contemplate running slow, vulnerable transports down the Slot in the face of

American air supremacy. Indeed for the time being they made no attempt to send reinforcements to Guadalcanal, being content to deliver supplies to their existing forces there by the 'Tokyo Expresses'.

This task was again entrusted to Rear-Admiral Tanaka's Destroyer Squadron 2. He planned to load his ships with sterilized metal drums containing food or medical supplies, with enough air space left to ensure buoyancy. These would be pushed overboard off the Japanese base at Tassafaronga, where they could be collected by small craft operating from the beach. This method would reduce the unloading time to a minimum, enabling Tanaka to be well away from the island when dawn brought its threat of air-attacks. On 27th November, Tanaka arrived at Buin at the southern end of Bougainville with eight destroyers, ready for his first attempt.

American interception of enemy signals had already warned Halsey – who had been promoted to Admiral on 26th November – that another 'Tokyo Express' run was imminent. He had therefore assembled a cruiser-destroyer unit, known as Task Force 67, at Espiritu Santo in order to oppose this and had entrusted the command to Rear-Admiral Kinkaid who had arrived by air on the 24th.

Kinkaid at once set to work to prepare a detailed battle plan which would ensure that the errors made in previous night fighting were not repeated. He was determined that accurate information of the enemy should be obtained as soon as possible, so directed that two picket destroyers should be sent some ten miles ahead of his main force to provide early warning. The cruisers' float-planes would be used as additional scouts and they would drop flares to illuminate the Japanese when required; the use of searchlights by American vessels was forbidden.

Nor did Kinkaid intend to adopt the long single column. He proposed that the remaining US destroyers should be stationed at 30 degrees on the engaged bow of the cruiser formation. From this position they would use their radar advantage to launch a surprise torpedo attack, after which they would turn away so as to avoid those possibilities of mistaken identity that had caused such problems in the past. The cruisers, which would try to remain at least 12,000 yards from the enemy, were not to open fire until the torpedoes had found their marks.

With this plan, which for the first time gave the American destroyers a chance of effective independent action, Kinkaid felt confident that he would be able to challenge Japanese supremacy at night. By 27th November, he had completed the details of his scheme. On the 28th, he was deprived of any chance of implementing it by an order from Nimitz directing him to Pearl Harbor, from which in due course he went to Dutch Harbor in the Aleutian Islands, where on 3rd January 1943, he assumed command of the North Pacific Force.

Since Kinkaid was a veteran with considerable experience of conditions in the Solomons, had just made the necessary preparations to deal with a specific, anticipated situation and was not called on to take up his new post immediately, it seems that his premature removal from the scene must be ranked as one of Nimitz's few mistakes. Even more strange was the fact that Halsey did not request Kinkaid's transfer to be postponed for a few days. His failure to intervene may in part have been due to differences in temperament. Kinkaid's may be summed up by a request he once made to newspaper correspondents : 'Please don't say I made any dramatic statements. You know I am incapable of that.' It would be hard to find an attitude less likely to be shared by Halsey.

In any case, Task Force 67 now became the responsibility of Rear-Admiral Carleton Wright, who had just reached Espiritu Santo in heavy cruiser *Minneapolis*. On 29th November, he held a hasty conference with the commanding officers of the five cruisers and four destroyers under his control. That evening, he was warned by Halsey – who in turn had received the information from the code-breakers – that a 'Toyko Express' was due to reach Ironbottom Sound on the following night. Task Force 67 duly put to sea. By dawn on the 30th, it was steering at high speed for Guadalcanal. The cruisers' float-planes were sent off to Tulagi, whence they were to seek out and if necessary illuminate the enemy warships.

At about the same time that Wright left Espiritu Santo, Tanaka sortied from Buin, setting a course to the north-east of the Solomons so as to escape the notice of American reconnaissance aircraft. At 1000 on the 30th, his lookouts sighted one such but to their surprise it continued on its course, having apparently seen nothing. However, Tanaka's departure was duly reported by coastwatchers, thus giving Wright confirmation that his foes were on their way.

Early in the afternoon, Tanaka entered a rain-storm, under cover of which he increased speed to 30 knots to race towards Guadalcanal. He also learned from Rabaul that American cruisers were approaching the island. As might have been expected, he was not seriously alarmed. Warning his captains of the 'great possibility of an encounter with the enemy tonight', he urged them not to employ gunfire which would give away their positions but to rely on torpedoes only, using the flashes from the American guns as their aiming-points.

Task Force 67 entered Ironbottom Sound at 2225 on 30th November, at a speed of 20 knots. The night was dark and overcast, with visibility about two miles. The sea was flat and calm. In Lengo Channel to the north-east of Guadalcanal, Wright had encountered three transports and five destroyers retiring from the area. On Halsey's orders two of the escort had joined the Task Force, though there was no time for Wright to notify them of the plan of operations or indeed give them detailed instructions of any sort.

Since Wright had approved of Kinkaid's plan, he had separated his vessels into two columns, with his four original destroyers stationed on the port bow of the cruisers and so nearest to the Japanese-held beach at Tassafaronga, though at 20 degrees not 30 degrees as suggested by Kinkaid. The leading destroyer was *Fletcher*, followed by *Perkins*, *Maury* and *Drayton* in that order. Wright's flagship, heavy cruiser *Minneapolis*, was two miles away from *Drayton*, at the head of the cruiser column in which the ships were 1,000 yards apart. Heavy cruiser *New Orleans* followed *Minneapolis*. Then came heavy cruiser *Pensacola*, light cruiser *Honolulu* flying the flag of Rear-Admiral Mahlon Tisdale, heavy cruiser *Northampton* and finally the two destroyers which had been detached from the convoy, *Lamson* and *Lardner*.

Unfortunately Wright had omitted one vital element of Kinkaid's scheme for he had not sent any of his destroyers in advance to give early warning. Nor could his float-planes, now temporarily based at Tulagi, rectify this error. The surface of the sea – described as 'like a black mirror' – was too calm for the pilots to get the 'lift' required for take-off. When finally they succeeded, it was too late.

At 2238, Wright altered course 40 degrees to port, all ships turning together, to steer directly for Tassafaronga in 'line of bearing' – that is in echelon. At 2306, the SG radar on *Minneapolis* revealed the presence of the enemy heading south-east at a distance of 23,000 yards. Wright at once ordered all his ships to turn 40 degrees to starboard together, thereby resuming his original two-column formation. Eight minutes later, however, he wheeled 20 degrees to port, parallel to the enemy's course, and formed his whole force into one single long column, just as Scott, Callaghan and Lee had done in earlier night actions. He thereby altered two more of the conditions laid down by Kinkaid. His destroyers were not stationed where their torpedoes would have a short run to their targets; his cruisers would be closer to the enemy than the 12,000 yards recommended.

Destroyer Squadron 2 of the Imperial Japanese Navy passed to the west of Savo Island at 2245. Tanaka flew his flag in the leading destroyer, *Naganami*. Destroyer *Takanami* was stationed some 2,000 yards on the flagship's port bow to act as a picket – these two vessels together being known as the Patrol Unit. Behind *Naganami* came Captain Torajiro Sato's Transport Unit 1 : *Makinami, Oyashio, Kuroshio* and *Kagero*. Bringing up the rear was Captain Giichiro Nakahara's Transport Unit 2 : *Kawakaze* and *Suzukaze*.

Of these vessels, only *Naganami* and *Takanami* carried no supplies so were ready for instant action. The decks of the remaining destroyers were cluttered with a total of 1,100 drums which obstructed their torpedo tubes. As the force neared Tassafaronga, Tanaka ordered speed reduced to 12 knots. In the Transport Units, the sailors began unlashing the drums, preparatory to casting them overboard. Thus preoccupied, they were totally unaware of the Americans' presence.

At 2316, Commander Cole of *Fletcher*, the senior captain in the van destroyers, called over the TBS for permission to fire torpedoes at the enemy, then clearly indicated on his SG radar. Unfortunately on the flagship's radar, Tanaka's destroyers had begun to merge with the nearby shoreline. Wright accordingly hesitated and every moment that he did so the range was increasing as the Japanese passed the Americans on an opposite course.

The best firing position had thus been lost but Wright could still have saved the situation by directing his destroyers to close the enemy in order to make their torpedo attack from short range. However, presumably fearing that this would lead to confusions in identity, he gave no such commands; nor was it until 2320, that he ordered Cole to 'go ahead and fire torpedoes' at all.

Of Cole's destroyers, *Maury*, equipped only with the SC radar, did

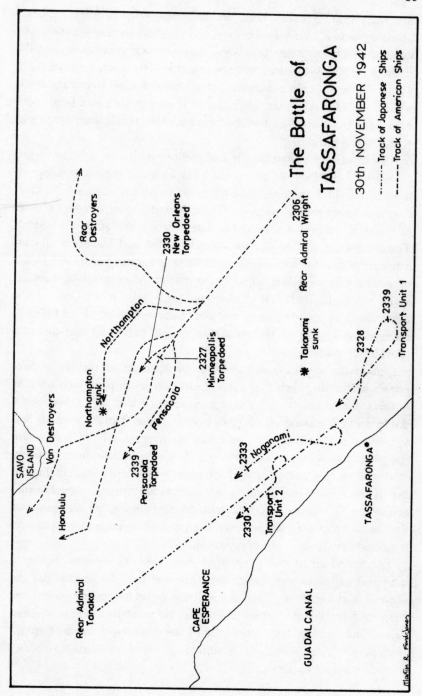

The Battle of
TASSAFARONGA

30th NOVEMBER 1942

----- Track of Japanese Ships
----- Track of American Ships

not fire, while *Drayton* launched only two of her 'fish'. *Fletcher*, however, sent off ten; *Perkins* eight. They had to travel over 9,500 yards to reach the main Japanese column, which greatly reduced the chances of hits, yet, since the enemy had slowed down and were still utterly ignorant of their danger, it is possible that the Americans could still have achieved at least some success if only gunfire had been withheld until the torpedoes had had a chance to reach their targets as Kinkaid had insisted.

Instead, the 'fish' had hardly commenced their run, when Wright, abandoning the last vestiges of the plan he had supposedly adopted, ordered his ships to commence firing. *Minneapolis* engaged the rival flagship *Naganami*. *Pensacola*, which lacked modern radar, was at first unable to find a target, but later turned her guns onto Sato's Transport Unit 1. *New Orleans, Northampton* and *Honolulu* all con-concentrated on the nearest enemy vessel, the hapless *Takanami*. Cole's four destroyers joined in, while at the rear of the cruiser line, *Lamson* and *Lardner* did their best to overcome the handicap of SC radar sets by shooting at any Japanese ship that became visible. In addition to the gunfire several of the American vessels also fired star-shells to provide illumination.

Caught by surprise and faced by this spectacular display of fire-power which they believed came from a battleship as well as four cruisers, the Japanese could have been excused had they fallen into a panic. In fact nothing was further from the case. Tanaka's vessels had long since determined upon and had often practised the manoeuvre they would adopt in such a situation. This was a simultaneous reversal of course by the leaders of each division, with the remaining ships of the division following them round, each vessel firing torpedoes independently. It was not easy to execute in daylight; in the darkness and the confusion of combat, not even the veterans of Destroyer Squadron 2 were able to carry it out as prescribed.

They performed well enough, however. *Takanami* promptly launched her torpedoes, then turned to starboard. *Naganami* did the same though without firing. Sato's four destroyers continued to the south-east for a time, while their crews desperately tried to hurl the drums into the sea, but at the rear of the Japanese column, Captain Nakahara's Transport Unit 2 turned to port, *Suzukaze* firing her torpedoes before doing so.

Nor, despite its impressiveness, was the American gunfire very effective. The star-shells did not reveal the enemy sufficiently clearly; the gunners were blinded by the blasts from their own weapons; it therefore proved difficult to locate targets. Indeed at 2325, Cole's destroyers lost track of Tanaka entirely and two minutes later retired towards Savo Island.

In consequence, although shells burst around *Naganami* as she turned, she received only minor damage from splinters, while all the vessels in the Transport Units escaped even this trivial harm. *Takanami*, however, between the two lines and under attack from three of Wright's cruisers, was hit repeatedly. In desperation she disregarded Tanaka's orders and began to use her own guns. This merely encouraged further American fire which quickly brought her to a standstill, flaming brightly and in a sinking condition.

Any elation that the Americans might have felt was short-lived. Wright had unwisely maintained a steady course and speed, his cruisers presenting easy marks for the torpedoes fired by *Takanami* and *Suzukaze*. At 2327, the 'Long Lances' began to strike back.

Flagship *Minneapolis* had just fired her ninth salvo, when two torpedoes crashed into her simultaneously. One wrecked her bow, some 60 feet of which was left hanging down below the water-line; the other exploded in a boiler-room. Fires sprang up with terrifying suddenness. Then two colossal pillars of water which had towered up to masthead height, smashed back onto the deck, sweeping two sailors overboard but miraculously quenching the flames. The flagship's speed fell away sharply, yet she fired three more full salvoes before all power was lost and she came almost to a halt.

Behind her, *New Orleans* swung sharply to starboard to avoid a collision. She was still turning when another 'Long Lance' hit her, detonating the forward magazine. A vast explosion blew off 120 feet of her bow, including the No 1 8-inch turret, and killed the crew of her No 2 turret as well. The detached forward part of the ship grated down her port side, tearing holes in her plating and damaging her propellers, before sinking. *New Orleans* also slowed to a crawl.

These catastrophes caused the American formation to disintegrate. *Pensacola* turned sharply to port, towards the enemy, so as to avoid the cripples. Light cruiser *Honolulu* and heavy cruiser *Northampton* swung away to starboard. Destroyers *Lamson* and *Lardner* tried to follow them but in the confusion they came under fire – luckily inaccurate – from the damaged cruisers, so wisely decided to withdraw to the north-east.

At this inauspicious moment, the float-planes, which had at last managed to take off, arrived overhead. Their powerful flares would have helped Task Force 67 immensely, yet they had been told to use these only if ordered. No instructions came from shattered *Minneapolis*, so no flares were dropped.

The Japanese destroyers needed no orders to use their weapons. *Kuroshio*, still moving south-east with the rest of Sato's ships, fired eight torpedoes at 2328. *Kawakaze* from Transport Unit 2 launched eight at 2330 and Tanaka's *Naganami* loosed her torpedoes three minutes later. At 2337, US destroyer *Drayton* also fired four torpedoes, aiming at *Naganami*, *Kawakaze* and *Suzukaze*, all of which by that time were heading north-west at high speed.

Drayton's 'fish' failed to find a target but as so often the Japanese were more successful. At 2339, a torpedo struck *Pensacola* amidships, causing heavy damage, flooding the after engine-room, knocking out three turrets and all communications, reducing the ship's speed to 8 knots and starting raging fires. Even the mast went up in flames, burning to death the wretched lookouts who were stationed there.

Captain Sato had by now turned his own vessel, *Makinami*, to starboard but before destroyer *Oyashio*, astern of him, commenced her turn, she fired eight torpedoes at 2339. She then reversed course more sharply than *Makinami*, losing touch with her as a result. *Kuroshio* followed *Oyashio* but *Kagero* at the rear of Sato's unit closed in upon *Makinami*. Both *Makinami* and *Kagero* then steered towards the Americans so as to reduce the range.

Meanwhile Captain Willard Kitts had brought heavy cruiser *Northampton*, still firing almost continuously, back onto a westerly course. It was a fatal decision. At 2348, two of the 'Long Lances' launched by *Oyashio* tore open her port side, bringing her to a halt, burning furiously and listing badly. Light cruiser *Honolulu* escaped the torpedoes, came under fire from the damaged American vessels, luckily without being hit, zig-zagged away to the north-west and eventually circled round Savo Island; as did Cole's destroyers.

The Battle of Tassafaronga, last major action in the struggle for Guadalcanal, was now virtually over. At 2352, *Makinami* and *Kagero* fired torpedoes at the injured heavy cruisers but, curiously enough, without success. *Oyashio* and *Kuroshio* returned to rescue most of the survivors from *Takanami*, which had now been abandoned, though she did not sink until 0137 on 1st December. By then, Tanaka's seven remaining destroyers were already speeding away from the danger-zone. They arrived safely at Shortland Island before noon.

Rear-Admiral Tisdale in *Honolulu*, to whom Wright now passed tactical command, spent the remainder of the night patrolling Iron-bottom Sound. The American destroyers gradually reassembled and moved to the aid of the vessels that had been torpedoed : *Lamson* and *Lardner* to *Minneapolis*; *Maury* to *New Orleans*; *Perkins* to *Pensa-cola*; *Fletcher* and *Drayton* to *Northampton*.

All four heavy cruisers were sorely stricken. If it had not been for the improvements in damage control made after and as a result of the Battle of Savo Island, every one would have been lost. As it was, the most desperate efforts could not save *Northampton*. By 0115, her list had increased to 23 degrees. Her men, except for Captain Kitts and a salvage party, began to abandon her. At 0240, she was lying over at 35 degrees and the remaining crew-members went over the side. At 0304, she vanished below the black waters. *Fletcher* and *Drayton* rescued 773 sailors; only 58 were lost.

The other injured ships made their way precariously towards Tulagi, eighteen miles away. *Minneapolis* and *New Orleans* were reduced to a crawl by their missing bows. On the former, the men in one fireroom stayed at their posts though compartments over them as well as around them were flooded. On the latter, poisonous gas entered the central damage control station. The three officers there, Lieutenant-Commander Hayter, Lieutenant Haines and Ensign For-man, got their men out but were overcome by the fumes before they could follow and all lost their lives. *Pensacola* was still ablaze, machine-gun ammunition was exploding and at 0145, the 8-inch shells in No 3 turret also began to blow up, though fortunately only one at a time over a period of some hours.

Yet not only did the cripples reach Tulagi but there, with only the limited resources of the PT-base available, they were again made sufficiently seaworthy to leave the combat area – *Minneapolis* and *New Orleans* wearing temporary bows made out of coconut logs. They all got to major bases where proper repairs could be carried out, though so severe were their injuries that nine months elapsed before any of them were again fit for action.

Apart from their admirable damage control, there were few aspects of this encounter from which the Americans could derive the slightest satisfaction. For all their superior numbers, their SG radars, their bitter experiences over the past four months, they still could not match their enemy at night. Even the lessons they had learned – at the cost of the services of vitally needed ships and 400 lives – were largely negative; the action, as Nimitz grimly remarked, merely 'provided a sort of textbook, later well studied', on how not to combat the 'Long Lance'.

The Imperial Navy had long considered that the surface torpedo attack exemplified its 'traditional qualities: skill, courage, surprise, daring and indifference to losses'. In the Battle of Tassafaronga, Tanaka's warriors had displayed all these qualities in abundance – save for the last which they had been too expert to need. Well might Japan be proud of her magnificent destroyers and their valiant, capable and devoted seamen.

CHAPTER EIGHT

Evacuation

Equal valour in the face of heavy odds was shown by the Japanese land forces on Guadalcanal, whose position was becoming more hopeless daily. The Americans were not only increasing their numbers but were able to withdraw exhausted units, replacing them with fresh fighting men. On 7th December, the soldiers of the 132nd Infantry Regiment came ashore. Two days later, Vandegrift handed over his command to Major-General Alexander Patch of the United States Army and the bulk of his First Marine Division at last sailed from the island on which it had achieved and endured so much. The remainder of the division left on the 22nd, apart from the men of the 7th Marine Regiment, who, it may be remembered, had not formed part of the original invasion force but had reached Guadalcanal on 18th September; they were evacuated on 5th January 1943.

The vessels on which the 7th Marine Regiment embarked had, on the previous day, landed a Regiment from the Second Marine Division, but the heaviest reinforcements arrived on 29th December, when three transports set ashore 7,737 officers and men of the 25th Infantry Division under Major-General Lawton Collins, together with 180 vehicles and 7,110 tons of cargo. A steady series of convoys kept the soldiers and Marines well supplied, while American transport aircraft brought in aviation fuel, ammunition, bombs and medical equipment, not by way of a desperate interim measure as in October, but as a regular supplement to the seaborne supply route.

While the flying transports were only temporary visitors, the number of aircraft permanently based on Guadalcanal continued to grow. By the end of December 'Cactus Air Force' contained 188 machines including nine Catalinas, painted black – hence their nickname of 'Black Cats' – and manned by crews specially trained to operate by

night. The American airmen gave constant support to their ground
troops; captured enemy diaries lament that they strafed or bombed
'every day' whereas Japanese aircraft were conspicuous by their
absence.

This was only one of Hyakutake's problems. He desperately needed
supplies of all kinds. Food was very low, even coconuts were running
short and thousands of Japanese troops were slowly dying of malnutrition. Ammunition was limited, particularly for the artillery pieces.
Medical equipment was so scarce that only those men who were
critically ill or wounded could be treated, the remainder being left to
recover as best they might.

Yet these ghastly conditions did not lessen the Japanese will to resist.
Although before the Naval Battle of Guadalcanal, they had been
engaged mainly in a series of attacks on the American positions, from
mid-November onwards, they had no option but to go onto the
defensive. In this new role, however, they soon showed that they
possessed considerable ability.

It was in fact in the last stages of the fighting on Guadalcanal that
the Japanese revealed that consummate skill in defence that was to be
come an outstanding feature of all subsequent campaigns in the Pacific.
'They seemed,' says Griffith, 'to have an instinctive feeling for terrain
(which Americans lack almost entirely).' Their ability to choose the best
sites for their machine-guns or their highly accurate and lethal 90-mm
mortars was almost uncanny. And, being an immensely artistic race,
they quickly proved to be past-masters of the art of camouflage. Their
defences simply could not be spotted from the air; frequently indeed
they were not located by troops on the ground until they had opened
fire.

Yet the greatest asset of the Japanese was that stubborn persistence
which made them fight on to the death in the most hopeless circumstances, rather than surrender. This dedication made every Japanese
platoon a battalion, every Japanese post a fortress. No wonder that an
Intelligence report, reviewing the Guadalcanal campaign, noted
grimly : 'All Japs must be shot at until dead and after that a shot or
two to make sure might not be ammunition wasted.'

In consequence, American progress throughout December continued
to be painfully slow. On the 17th, Patch launched an assault against
Mount Austen, a series of grass-covered ridges just over three miles

south-west of Henderson Field. Unfortunately, preliminary reconnaissance proved to have been inadequate, Japanese defences proved to have been sited with immense skill and bombing attacks and artillery bombardments against them proved to have been largely a waste of time. On the 24th, the highest point on the ridges, where the enemy had had an observation post, was captured but the main Japanese position, which was named the 'Gifu' after a prefecture in Japan's largest island, Honshu, defied all attacks. By 2nd January, the Americans were forced to suspend operations, having incurred heavy casualties for the minimum of results.

Hyakutake had succeeded admirably in his task of holding firm until his superiors could arrange a new offensive. This the Japanese still had every intention of mounting in mid-January. As part of their preparations for it, they had commenced on 24th November, to build a new airfield at Munda, New Georgia, only 175 miles from Henderson Field.

Here also Japanese camouflage was almost perfect. The site chosen for the airstrip was a coconut grove. Under the protection of the trees, work commenced at a furious rate. When a tree had to be felled, the Japanese erected palm-fronds on overhead wires in the exact position in which it had stood. It was not until 5th December that aerial photographs, skilfully interpreted, revealed the truth. Bombing raids commenced almost at once but by the 12th, the airfield was ready and some 30 Zeros were stationed thereon.

Pending completion of the Munda airstrip, Zeros from the Japanese bases in the northern Solomons provided cover for the 'Tokyo Expresses' which came to deliver supplies to Hyakutake's troops. There were three of these in December and as a result of their previous victory at Tassafaronga, the enemy vessels, though threatened by air attacks during the day, were opposed at night only by PT-boats.

It is unfortunate that due to subsequent events, the best-known PT attack of the war is one in Blackett Strait on the night of 1/2nd August 1943, when fifteen of them attempted to ambush a small enemy force of destroyers carrying troops. Morison describes the action thus: 'They used torpedoes lavishly but made not one hit on enemy ships going or coming.' As a culmination of this unsuccessful interception, *PT-109* commanded by a certain Lieutenant John F. Kennedy was deliberately rammed, not even fired upon, by an enemy destroyer while at slow speed. This encounter, which has attracted such admiration since, cost Kennedy his ship, cut clean in half, and two of his crew their lives, but Commander Hanami of *Amagiri* merely the tip of a propeller-blade. The actions of the PT-boats against the 'Tokyo Expresses' at Guadalcanal were far more worthy of attention.

Regrettably, however, when ten destroyers headed for Guadalcanal on 3rd December, the motor-torpedo-boats did not engage them, though the 'Cactus Air Force' made a bomb-hit which caused minor damage to *Makinami* and shot down three escorting Zeros at the cost of two American aircraft destroyed. The Japanese pressed on, to drop 1,500 drums of supplies off Tassafaronga. Yet only 310 of these were brought ashore by the exhausted soldiers before daylight and the remainder were then sunk by machine-gun fire from US fighters.

The 'Tokyo Express' of 7th December had a warmer reception. The eleven destroyers, led by Captain Torajiro Sato who had commanded Transport Unit 1 at Tassafaronga, were first attacked from the air. A near-miss on *Nowake* killed seventeen men and resulted in such serious flooding that she had to turn back, escorted by three of her comrades. In the course of the raid, however, Guadalcanal's leading dive-bomber pilot, Major Joseph Sailer, lost his life.*

Sato's remaining ships reached Ironbottom Sound safely but were then engaged by four PT-boats. During the action, *PT-59*, commanded by Lieutenant Searles, approached to within 100 yards of *Oyashio*. That redoubtable destroyer – which had sunk *Northampton* at Tassafaronga – scored ten hits on the PT-boat but Searles managed to coax his battered craft back to Tulagi. None of the PT-boats' torpedoes found a target, but they managed to avoid being rammed, they did considerable damage with their machine-guns and best of all they forced the Japanese to retire without delivering any supplies whatever.

Further success attended the motor-torpedo-boats' efforts when the next 'Tokyo Express' arrived on 11th December. Of the ten destroyers which took part, nine only carried supplies. *Terutsuki*, flying the flag of the valiant Raizo Tanaka, was entrusted with the task of preventing

* During his service on Guadalcanal, Sailer had led his Dauntlesses on 25 combat missions, of which 19 had resulted in attacks being made. In the course of these, he had personally made 6 direct-hits and at least 3 damaging near-misses.

any interference by the PT-boats. At sunset, Tanaka's force was attacked by fourteen dive-bombers, suitably escorted, but escaped without damage. The supply destroyers subsequently dropped another 1,200 drums off Cape Esperance, though again by no means all of these found their way to the Japanese ashore.

While this was taking place, Tanaka was fighting off the PT-boats. At 0100 on 12th December, at least one, probably two torpedoes from Lieutenant Gamble's *PT-45* crashed into *Terutsuki*. Tanaka was slightly wounded and knocked unconscious and his flagship came to a halt, on fire, in a sinking condition.

Destroyers *Naganami* and *Arashi* quickly arrived to rescue survivors. They took off Tanaka and a number of others but were then subjected to more attacks. *PT-44* received several direct hits that sank her almost instantly with the loss of all except two of her crew, but the Japanese destroyers, which clearly had a healthy respect for their little opponents, retired without completing their task. At 0440, *Terutsuki*'s fires reached a magazine and she exploded.

The loss of another valuable destroyer and the prospective loss of others so alarmed the Japanese that they did not order out any more 'Tokyo Expresses' during December.* They attempted to drop food from low-flying Bettys but these suffered heavy casualties without achieving any practical results, so that scheme also was abandoned. In consequence the Imperial Navy was forced to adopt the wasteful method of supplying the Guadalcanal garrison by means of submarines.

During December 1942 and January 1943, more than twenty 'I-boats' were employed on such work but again there was a price to be paid. On 9th December, *PT-59*, only just patched-up from injuries received in her clash with the 'Tokyo Express' two days earlier, sighted *I-3* on the surface and promptly sank her with two torpedoes, killing all except one of her crew. On 29th January *I-1* was attacked by two 600-ton minesweepers of the Royal New Zealand Navy, *Kiwi* and *Moa*. The former rammed the submarine – which was bigger than she was – three times. Both poured gunfire into her. *I-1* was finally

---

* However, they did send convoys to Munda, which resulted in further injuries to their destroyers. *Uzuki* was damaged by a collision with transport *Nankai Maru* during a submarine attack on 25th December. *Kagero* and *Ariake* were damaged by air-strikes on 16th and 26th December respectively.

driven onto a reef, whence she slid to the bottom leaving her bow sticking up out of the water. Again only one survivor was rescued.*

While the Japanese submarines were reduced to this secondary role, American submarines were becoming increasingly active in the waters around the Solomons. Unlike their Japanese counterparts, they concentrated on sinking enemy merchantmen. This was less spectacular than attacks on warships but in some ways even more effective. Already Japan was suffering from the mounting casualties among her cargo vessels. The reason why she had gone to war in the first place was to secure vital raw materials but it was now becoming ever more difficult to bring these from her newly-won territories to the war industries in the homeland and to carry reinforcements or supplies to preserve her conquests from the threat of counter-attack. Nor did Japan have sufficient industrial strength to make good her unexpectedly high shipping losses.

Thus during December, a number of factors combined to make it clear to Imperial General Headquarters that the cost of continuing the Guadalcanal campaign had become prohibitive. Yamamoto had wished to abandon the island ever since the great naval battle in mid-November. After the loss of *Terutsuki*, even the stout-hearted Tanaka felt that it was pointless to fight on any longer. He was relieved as Commander, Reinforcement Force by Rear-Admiral Koniji Koyanagi and on 29th December, returned to Japan for a period of recuperation.† Perhaps the issue was finally decided by a signal from Hyakutake on 23rd December, asking permission – which was refused – for a suicide assault on the American defences so as to meet an 'honourable death' rather than one from hunger.

On 31st December therefore, the Emperor gave his formal approval for the Japanese garrison on Guadalcanal to be withdrawn. Four days later, official orders to this effect were flown to Rabaul.

Meanwhile on 2nd January, a 'Tokyo Express' of ten destroyers came down the Slot. It was sighted by Flying Fortresses but their attacks were unsuccessful. A Dauntless raid just before nightfall

---

* The Americans later salvaged a number of vital secret documents from *I-1* but too late for these to be of use in the final rounds of the struggle for Guadalcanal.

† Morison mistakenly reports that Tanaka commanded the January missions of the 'Tokyo Express' – possibly out of force of habit.

damaged *Suzukaze*. Eleven PT-boats engaged the enemy after dark but this time without results. However, next day the motor-torpedo-boats found the drums that the Japanese had unloaded and sank them with machine-gun fire.

The night of 10/11th January saw another clash between eight PT-boats and a similar number of Japanese destroyers. Honours may be considered about even. *PT-43* and *PT-112* were both sunk by gunfire but their crews escaped on life-rafts without the loss of a man. Destroyer *Hatsukaze* was struck by a torpedo which caused consider-able damage but she was able to withdraw safely. In the morning, the PT-boats again 'held target practice' on the supply-drums.

A more important 'Tokyo Express' arrived on the pitch-black night of the 14/15th. Since it was too dark for the PT-boats to hope to make successful interceptions save by sheer good fortune, only a few spas-modic encounters took place which resulted in no harm being done to either side. The nine Japanese destroyers put ashore 600 men under Colonel Matsuda who were to act as a rearguard for the planned withdrawal. Early next day, fifteen Dauntlesses with a fighter escort attacked the retiring enemy but inflicted only minor injuries on *Arashi* and *Urakaze*.

Among the officers who reached Guadalcanal on this occasion was Lieutenant-Colonel Imoto, who had been given the unpleasant task of informing Hyakutake of the decision to abandon the island. When he heard the news, Hyakutake, who had believed that the arrival of the reinforcements had heralded a future offensive, asked to be left alone to consider the matter. After spending all morning in thought, he announced that he would 'respectfully comply with the conditions of the order'. The commanders of the 2nd and 38th Divisions, Lieu-tenant-Generals Maruyama and Sano, were then notified. They too stated that they would 'abide by the decision'.

Only the senior Japanese commanders and their principal staff officers were informed of the proposed evacuation; the bulk of the troops being told that they were being redeployed for future operations. The Americans were kept equally in ignorance of their enemy's deci-sion since on the first day of 1943, the Japanese made major changes in their codes which the American cryptanalysts were not able to break in time to be of value. On 10th January therefore, Patch began a new offensive, his principal objectives being the 'Gifu' position and two neighbouring hills known as 'Sea Horse' and 'Galloping Horse' from their resemblance to these creatures on aerial photographs.

Considering the exhaustion of the defenders, American progress was again disappointing. On 13th January, 'Galloping Horse' was captured; Captain Charles Davis winning a Congressional Medal of Honor while leading an attack against a machine-gun emplacement. 'Sea Horse' fell three days later, but the 'Gifu', though completely surrounded, still held out. Appeals to the Japanese to surrender were, needless to say, ignored. Resistance continued until the night of 21/22nd January, when, led by their commander Major Inagaki, the remaining enemy soldiers, about 100 in number, charged into the American lines to meet their deaths.

By this time of course Hyakutake had received his orders to withdraw. His men fell back slowly, pursued by the Americans, whose advance along the coast was greatly aided by naval gunfire. On the 19th, destroyers *Nicholas*, *O'Bannon*, *Radford* and *DeHaven* each expended between 500 and 600 5-inch shells against enemy shore positions. The Japanese base at Kokumbona fell on the 23rd. On the 26th, destroyer *Fletcher* executed a highly successful bombardment, much to the admiration of Patch who was on board her to watch this, while three days later, *Anderson* and *Wilson* achieved similar satisfactory results.

The US Navy was also using its guns against targets farther afield. On the night of 4/5th January, a squadron under Rear-Admiral Walden Ainsworth headed for Munda. Heavy cruiser *Louisville*, light cruisers *Honolulu*, *Columbia* and HMNZS *Achilles* (of River Plate fame), and destroyers *Drayton*, *Lamson* and *Nicholas* manoeuvred to the south-east to provide support, while light cruisers *Nashville* (Ainsworth's flagship), *St Louis* and *Helena* and destroyers *Fletcher* and *O'Bannon* prepared to bombard the new airfield and 'Black Cats' flew overhead to spot fall of shot.

For 50 minutes commencing at 0100 on the 5th, Ainsworth's ships hurled nearly 3,000 6-inch and some 1,400 5-inch shells into Munda. Fires sprang up; debris flew in all directions; trees came crashing to the ground. Yet the damage was more spectacular than real. By noon on the same day, the Japanese had repaired the runway sufficiently to render it operational again.

Furthermore as the Allied formation was retiring to the south of

Guadalcanal, four Vals made a surprise attack out of the sun. Three bombs which near-missed *Honolulu* did no harm but a direct hit on *Achilles* killed thirteen men, wounded eight more and so wrecked No 3 turret that she had to journey as far as England in order to have a new one fitted.

On the night of 23/24th January, Ainsworth organized another bombardment, this time of an air-strip which the Japanese were constructing at Vila in the south of Kolombangara Island. The pattern of the raid was similar to that on Munda. *Honolulu* and *St Louis*, guarded by destroyers *Drayton*, *Lamson* and *Hughes*, formed the support group, while *Nashville* and *Helena*, escorted by destroyers *Nicholas*, *O'Bannon*, *Radford* and *DeHaven*, and directed by 'Black Cats', fired nearly 2,000 6-inch and some 1,500 5-inch shells in a half-hour period commencing at 0200. The damage was increased during a raid by 24 Dauntlesses, 17 Avengers and 18 Wildcats from Henderson Field at 0800 – but again the hard-working Japanese made it good in a remarkably short time. Ainsworth's vessels were again subjected to an air-raid, on this occasion at night, but they escaped unscathed and shot down one of their attackers.

By now aerial reconnaissance had reported a massive concentration of Japanese warships at or near Rabaul. These were preparing for the evacuation of Guadalcanal but Halsey thought that a reinforcement of the island was intended. Since he also planned to send in troops and supplies on four transports which were due to reach Guadalcanal on the 30th, he determined that these would have an escort sufficiently strong to crush any Japanese interference that might develop.

In all, Halsey's fleet comprised carriers *Enterprise* and *Saratoga* (newly returned to the South Pacific having made good her battle-damage), escort carriers *Chenango* and *Suwanee*, battleships *Washington*, *North Carolina* (also back with repairs completed) and *Indiana*, 12 cruisers and 25 destroyers. However, most of these vessels steamed at least 250 miles behind the transports and their close-support group, which was commanded by Rear-Admiral Robert Giffen and consisted of the two escort carriers, heavy cruisers *Wichita* (flagship), *Chicago* and *Louisville*, light cruisers *Montpelier*, *Cleveland* and *Columbia* and destroyers *LaVallette*, *Waller*, *Conway*, *Frazier*, *Chevalier*, *Edwards*, *Meade* and *Taylor*.

Giffen had just reached the area after service in the Atlantic, which had taught him that submarines rather than aircraft were the major threat. In consequence, when he found that the slow speed of his escort carriers would prevent him from reaching Guadalcanal on schedule, he felt no concern about leaving them to proceed separately, escorted by *Frazier* and *Meade*, while he pushed on at 24 knots with the bulk of his force. The escort carriers provided a combat air patrol during the daylight hours but the American airmen had retired by the time the sun set at 1850 on 29th January.

Giffen was then about 50 miles north of Rennell Island, heading north-west. His cruisers steamed in two columns, 2,500 yards apart, the light cruisers to port, the heavy cruisers to starboard. The destroyers formed a semicircle two miles ahead. These dispositions were adequate to counter submarines but ill-suited to meet air-attacks. Nor had Giffen issued any orders as to the action to be taken if such attacks should commence.

This was regrettable because during the afternoon, Yamamoto had dispatched 31 torpedo-carrying Bettys from Munda airfield with orders to destroy Giffen's ships. They arrived soon after dark, to begin a series of raids with the help of highly-effective parachute flares.

The Japanese torpedoes proved less effective than usual in this encounter : both *Wichita* and *Louisville* were hit by ones that did not explode. The Japanese airmen suffered heavy losses but ironically it was one of these which enabled them to record their only success. At about 1940, an aircraft in flames crashed just off *Chicago*'s port bow, illuminating her brightly. Several Bettys raced towards this obvious target and two torpedoes tore open her starboard side, jamming her rudder, causing an 11-degree list and flooding an engine-room and two firerooms which brought her to a halt.

Heavy cruiser *Louisville* took the injured vessel in tow – a splendid feat of seamanship in pitch-blackness – and by dawn on 30th January, *Chicago* was moving towards Espiritu Santo at a painful 4 knots. Tug *Navajo*, accompanied by destroyer-transport *Sands*, arrived to take over the tow. A task force, including *Enterprise*, closed to within some 45 miles of *Chicago* to provide air cover. Giffen's remaining cruisers left the area at 1500, but his destroyers stayed behind, circling protectively around the cripple.

It seemed that *Chicago* might still be saved but it was not to be. During the morning, two enemy scouts sighted her and escaped. At

1540, four Wildcats from *Enterprise* detected a Betty which they managed to shoot down after a 40-mile chase. Their departure in pursuit, however, meant that only six fighters were available when at 1554, *Enterprise*'s radar warned of an advancing raid of twelve more Bettys armed with torpedoes.

The Japanese airmen had originally intended that the carrier would be their target but when at about 1615, they were engaged by the defending fighters, they quickly reversed course to the north to assault *Chicago* which they had sighted a few minutes earlier. The Wildcats were able to down only three of them and four more fighters which had been covering Giffen's cruisers but now raced to the scene, were unable to intercept in time.

At about 1620, the nine remaining Bettys burst out of the clouds. Anti-aircraft fire and fighters shot down all except two of them, yet most, if not all, got their torpedoes away first. One hit destroyer *LaVallette* in the forward engine-room but she was able to reach Espiritu Santo with the aid of a tow. Four smashed into *Chicago*'s already damaged starboard side. She sank twenty minutes later.*

Meanwhile the American transports had delivered their men and equipment safely, as did another convoy of five transports on 4th February. By then in any case, reinforcements were no longer required.

Major-General Patch, who, like Halsey, believed that the Japanese were planning a major offensive, had suspended operations until the convoy of 30th January had reached him. On 1st February, he resumed his westward advance and on the same day, destroyer-transport *Stringham* and five LCTs† carried troops, supplies and artillery under Lieutenant-Colonel George to Verahue near the north-west extremity of Guadalcanal, from which they could execute a pincer movement towards Cape Esperance.

George's men were protected by destroyers *Fletcher*, *Radford*, *Nicholas* and *DeHaven*. The landing proved free of problems but on their return to Ironbottom Sound, *Nicholas* and *DeHaven* were attacked by dive-bombers. The former, which was the target for eight aircraft, escaped with near-misses that killed two men and damaged

---

* This series of air-attacks on 29th and 30th January has been dignified with the title of 'The Battle of Rennell Island'.

† The initials stood for 'Landing Craft, Tank'.

the steering-gear, but the six Vals which assaulted *DeHaven* scored three direct hits and one very near miss, sinking the destroyer in less than 2 minutes, with the loss of 167 of her crew, including Commander Tolman.

Japanese reactions had been particularly violent because they had chosen the night of 1/2nd February for the first of their main evacuations.* American reconnaissance aircraft reported 20 destroyers racing down the Slot at high speed. To Halsey this looked like a big reinforcement mission. He gave orders that it must be stopped at all costs.

Fortunately for the Japanese seamen, their victory at the Battle of Tassafaronga had produced such a profound effect that not even the normally aggressive Halsey risked sending major warships against them after dark during any of their January or February operations. However, this first evacuation mission faced considerable perils from other forms of defence, including 255 mines which the Americans had laid across their enemy's most probable line of advance.

The main opponents of the 'Tokyo Express' were, as usual, the 'Cactus Air Force' and the PT-boats. The former made its appearance at 1820, when seventeen Dauntlesses and seven Avengers, accompanied by seventeen Wildcats, engaged the destroyers but were attacked in their turn by a protecting screen of Zero fighters. The destruction of four American aircraft was partially redeemed by a bomb-hit on *Makinami* which brought her to a halt. Leaving her crew fighting to keep her afloat – successfully as it transpired – the remaining nineteen vessels continued on their way. A raid by six more dive-bombers after dark was ineffective.

Nor did the PT-boats enjoy a reward worthy of their courage. *PT-37* and *PT-111* were sunk by gunfire, while *PT-123* had the singular misfortune of being hit by one of a number of Japanese bombers that were prowling above their destroyers in case American warships should intervene. The little boat, in Morison's words, 'disintegrated into flaming splinters'.

None of the PT-boats' torpedoes found a target but indirectly they again left their mark on the enemy. Destroyer *Makigumo*, manoeuvring to avoid their weapons, ran into the new minefield. An underwater explosion left her crippled and in flames. She had to be scuttled.

Eighteen destroyers reached Cape Esperance, where they took

* Small numbers of men had already been shipped out in barges or submarines.

aboard nearly 5,000 men, including the remnants of Sano's 38th Division. They then withdrew, escaping undamaged from another air-raid soon after dawn. On their return journey, they met up with *Makinami* and towed her to safety.

Thus encouraged, some twenty destroyers came down the Slot on 4th February. 'Cactus Air Force' sent 33 bombers and 31 fighters to meet them but the escorting Zeros or the ships' AA gunners shot down ten of these. The Wildcats claimed seventeen Japanese fighters but the American bombers had little effect, causing only minor damage to *Shiranuhi* and more serious damage to *Maikaze*. The PT-boats failed to intercept the enemy on this occasion and night-attacks by five Dauntlesses were unsuccessful.

This 'Tokyo Express' rescued the bulk of Maruyama's 'Sendai' Division – about 4,000 men – as well as most of the leading Japanese officers on the island. Among these was Hyakutake. Boarding destroyer *Hamakaze*, he hurried to his cabin, not once looking back at the lost island.

Finally on the 7th, eighteen destroyers carried out the last Japanese mission to Guadalcanal. Like the previous ones, it was harried by air-strikes. Bad weather prevented more than fifteen dive-bombers from finding the enemy. These claimed hits on *Hamakaze* and *Isokaze* but both remained in formation. That night a 2,000-strong rearguard led by Colonel Matsuda was evacuated.

Almost 11,000 men were rescued in the three big February missions, though some 600 of these died later of sickness or their injuries. This brilliant operation added a sour taste to the Americans' conquest of the island. They only realized what had happened when, during 8th and 9th February, their pincer movement closed in on nothing more than wrecked and abandoned equipment.

The Guadalcanal campaign was over. It had lasted for exactly six months.

CHAPTER NINE

Vengeance

On the afternoon of 17th April 1943, Major John Mitchell and Captain Thomas Lanphier, the two senior officers of the 339th Fighter Squadron of the United States Army Air Force, based at Henderson Field, Guadalcanal, with Lockheed Lightnings, were handed a top-secret dispatch. It had been sent by Frank Knox, Secretary of the Navy, who was acting on information from Nimitz, who in turn had received it from his code-breakers – though for security reasons, a 'cover story' was put out giving the credit to nameless Australian coastwatchers. The pilots set to work planning the details of the operation with which they had been entrusted. That evening, four Liberators arrived from Port Moresby with auxiliary tanks which would provide the fighters with sufficient fuel for a 435-mile flight to the target-zone.

All through the night, the fitters toiled in torrential rain to equip eighteen Lightnings with their tanks, while the men who would take them into action tried to get some sleep. By dawn the storm had passed; the morning was bright and clear. At 0725 on 18th April, the aircraft left Henderson Field but two of them suffered mishaps on take-off which reduced the force to sixteen.

The Americans flew at low level to avoid detection by the enemy's radar. At 0934, they were approaching the southern tip of Bougainville from the west. A shout from Lieutenant Canning broke the radio-silence as he sighted two Bettys escorted by six Zeros flying south along the coast five miles away. The pilots were slightly surprised – they had expected to see only one Betty and six Zeros. Dropping their auxiliary tanks, they prepared to attack.

Lanphier made for the leading Betty. He shot down a Zero which tried to intervene; then caught up with his target as it dodged away over the jungle at low level. As he reported later :

I fired a long steady burst across the bomber's course of flight, from approximately right angles. The bomber's right engine, then its right wing burst into flame.

It plunged through the trees, leaving a column of black smoke to mark its destruction. Lanphier's Lightning received only two minor hits in its rudder, though he considered that he had also lost 'a year or two off my life'.

Lieutenant Barber brought down the other Betty, which crashed in shallow water just off the coast. Lieutenant Holmes destroyed two more Zeros but Lieutenant Hine was shot down and killed. The remaining fifteen Lightnings returned in triumph to Guadalcanal.

Among the Japanese officers who lost their lives in this encounter were Surgeon Rear-Admiral Takata, Commanders Toibana and Muroi who were considered the two 'brains' of the Imperial Navy's air staff, and Admiral Isoroku Yamamoto the Navy's Commander-in-Chief. Next day, a rescue force, hacking its way through the jungle, found the Admiral's body. Yamamoto was still in his seat, which had been thrown clear of the wrecked aircraft, still gripping his sword in his left hand. There were bullet-holes through his skull and shoulder. Vice-Admiral Matome Ugaki, the Chief of Staff, escaped from the second Betty, seriously injured. The Americans had code-named the mission : Operation 'Vengeance'.

'To the Japanese Navy,' proclaimed Admiral Nimitz later, 'the loss of its most able and colourful commander was the equivalent of a major defeat.' His successor, Admiral Mineichi Koga, admitted that : 'There was only one Yamamoto and no one is able to replace him. His loss is an insupportable blow to us.'

It has often been pointed out how ironical it was that Yamamoto should have been killed by aircraft operating from Guadalcanal, which he had formerly made such efforts to subdue, yet the extreme appropriateness of his death at the hands of pilots based on that island has attracted less notice. 'The Admiral's destruction', as Ronald Lewin states in *The Other Ultra*,* 'was a symbolic episode in the history of the war in the Pacific' : for the death of its Commander-in-Chief foreshadowed the destruction of the Imperial Navy.

* This book deals with the information gained by the Americans from their ability to break the Japanese codes.

Yet in reality this had already been foreshadowed by the American conquest of Guadalcanal, although this was scarcely appreciated at the time. In strategic terms, the importance of the conquest was obvious. Guadalcanal with its crucial airfield was the key to the southern Solomons. When the Japanese lost it, they lost also their initiative in the south Pacific. Their threat to the main Allied bases in general and to the vital supply lines to Australia and New Zealand in particular was finally eliminated. On the contrary, the Americans had gained an advance base from which they could strike, first against the central and northern Solomons, then into the heart of Japan's newly-conquered territories. The fall of Guadalcanal marked the moment when the Americans went onto the offensive, which they were never again to relinquish.

The fighting on land had also ended very much in favour of the Americans. Not only did the soldiers and Marines gain valuable moral benefits from the knowledge that they could beat the Japanese even on their own ground in jungle conditions, but of the 60,000 men committed, the casualties amounted only to 1,592 killed, 4,709 wounded – though few indeed of those who served on the island escaped the ravages of malaria. Of the 36,000 Japanese who fought on Guadalcanal, about 23,800 died in combat or of disease and about 1,000 were taken prisoner. No wonder that the Imperial Army referred to Guadalcanal as the 'Island of Death'.

Yet before the American ground-troops could kill Japanese soldiers or capture Japanese bases, the United States Navy had to convey them to their target, ensure that the food, weapons, ammunition, fuel, medical supplies and equipment of all kinds that they needed were brought to them, and prevent the enemy from taking advantage of his internal lines of communication to build up the defences of the threatened area. Furthermore the Americans had to re-conquer a quite vast area. If it took six months to capture Guadalcanal, how long might it be before the Japanese homeland could be invaded? There appeared to be a terrible prospect that the fighting might last for years while a fanatical enemy took merciless and mammoth toll of the flower of American manhood.

For during the fighting for Guadalcanal, the American Navy – or, since Australian and New Zealand vessels had also fought and suffered, it would perhaps be more accurate to say the Allied Navies – had not shown anything like the superiority of the Army or Marine Corps. They had lost a total of 24 major warships in the course of the campaign :

2 Fleet Carriers : *Wasp*; *Hornet*.

6 Heavy Cruisers : *Canberra*; *Astoria*; *Quincy*; *Vincennes*; *North-hampton*; *Chicago*.

2 Light Cruisers : *Atlanta*; *Juneau*.

14 Destroyers : *Jarvis*; *Blue*; *O'Brien*; *Duncan*; *Meredith*; *Porter*; *Cushing*; *Laffey*; *Barton*; *Monssen*; *Walke*; *Preston*; *Benham*; *De-Haven*.

Japanese losses amounted to 18 major warships :

1 Light Carrier : *Ryujo*.

2 Battleships : *Hiei*; *Kirishima*.

3 Heavy Cruisers : *Kako*; *Furutaka*; *Kinugasa*.

1 Light Cruiser : *Yura*.

11 Destroyers : *Mutsuki*; *Asagiri*; *Fubuki*; *Murakumo*; *Natsugumo*; *Akatsuki*; *Yudachi*; *Ayanami*; *Takanami*; *Terutsuki*; *Makigumo*.

In tonnage sunk, both sides suffered almost equally, though nearly half the Japanese figure was represented by their two battleships, whose loss was less important than that of their two carriers was to the Americans. The human casualties on the sunken ships or those which survived badly damaged were never calculated by either side but were probably much the same.

It was impossible for the Americans to deny that they had been defeated in several of the naval actions fought around Guadalcanal; in two of them – Savo Island and Tassafaronga – humiliatingly defeated. Halsey might belittle his foes but most other commanders were only too well aware of their abilities. Despite his victory in the Naval Battle of Guadalcanal, Rear-Admiral Lee felt compelled to report that : 'our margin of superiority was due almost entirely to our possession of radar. Certainly we have no edge on the Japs in experience, skill, training or permanence of personnel'. After Tassafaronga, Nimitz did not hesitate to praise the enemy's 'energy, persistence and courage'. Even the evacuation emphasized Japanese abilities – in particular, to quote Nimitz again, their 'skill in keeping their plans disguised and bold celerity in carrying them out'.

Fortunately for the Americans, they had achieved a number of successes, the value of which would only become apparent later. The destruction of six enemy submarines – *I-1*, *I-3*, *I-15*, *I-22*, *I-123* and *I-172* – was probably less important than has been made out, if only because the Japanese never did make full use of these craft, but the heavy casualties among Japanese transports delivered a blow against the enemy compared to which the sinking of the US destroyer-transports *Colhoun*, *Little* and *Gregory* was insignificant.

During the Guadalcanal campaign, Japan's Merchant Marine lost about 300,000 tons of shipping – nearly 75,000 tons of it in the disaster to the great reinforcement convoy bringing the 38th Division to the island on 14th–15th November. Not only were several thousand more soldiers killed on the sunken vessels, to add to the casualties in the fighting on land, but, as has been mentioned earlier, the decline in Japan's transport strength meant that vital raw materials could not be brought back to the homeland.

Indeed a vicious circle was starting to develop which Japan had no power to break. Because of the loss of her merchantmen she began to suffer from a shortage of raw materials. Therefore she could not build new ships to replace those that had been sunk. Therefore she received still fewer imports. Lack of vessels also meant that those in service had to be used more frequently, thereby increasing maintenance problems. The same difficulties drastically reduced the production of warships. The Imperial Navy might have suffered fewer losses in the Guadalcanal campaign but they were losses which the Japanese shipyards would find almost impossible to replace.

The Americans by contrast were producing warships in increasing numbers. During 1943, 398 destroyers or the smaller destroyer-escorts were launched; Japan launched only nine. Battleship *Iowa* was commissioned in February 1943. On 31st December 1942, fleet carrier *Essex* of 27,100 tons, capable of operating up to 110 aircraft was commissioned. By the autumn of 1943, five sister-ships were serving with the Pacific Fleet. So were five light carriers of 11,000 tons operating 31–33 aircraft; the first of these, *Independence*, had been completed in January. 25 escort carriers were built during 1943. The Imperial Navy in that year received only three new 'flat-tops'; two former liners, *Shinyo* and *Kaiyo*, which, being too slow to operate with the fleet, were used for ferrying aircraft to overseas bases, and *Chiyoda*, a seaplane-tender converted, like her sister-ship *Chitose*, to a light carrier.

At the same time the Americans were able to show a really awesome production of cargo vessels. In March 1943 for example, they launched 140 7,157-ton 'Liberty Ships', each of which had taken fifteen days to build. Neither Japan nor any other country could hope to approach this achievement.

Nor was it only the Japanese Merchant Navy that had suffered severely at Guadalcanal; so had the Japanese Naval Air Force. During the campaign in combat or on operations it had lost 893 machines (carrier-based and land-based) and 2,362 men.

The Americans had also incurred heavy losses of aircraft but many of these had been wrecked on the ground as a result of bombardments. The casualties among their airmen, though never calculated exactly, were far less than those of the Japanese, partly because American machines, being more strongly built, could endure greater punishment; partly because American air-sea rescue operations were so highly effective. The Americans could also replace their losses more easily. Japan never had more than 4,000 naval pilots available but by December 1942, the US Navy could report that over 31,000 pilots were in training; while in 1943, American aircraft production was five times greater than that of Japan.

Alongside the growing American strength came an improvement in American weapons. Existing defects were remedied; thus by the end of 1943, the Americans had at last rectified the faults in their torpedoes. New technical advances were introduced; January 1943 for instance saw the first use by the Allies of the proximity-fused AA shell, which by means of a miniature radar set in its nose reflecting signals off solid objects such as aircraft, detonated automatically in the vicinity of its target when the intervals between the outward and returning signals became very short. This eventually proved so deadly that the Japanese airmen were reduced to suicide tactics in order to hit American warships.

Similar improvements took place in the air. In September 1942, the first Marine squadron equipped with the Chance-Vought Corsair was formed. The Corsair was used at first only from land-bases due to a poor deck-landing capability and did not serve on US carriers until early 1945.* The Grumman Hellcat, in contrast, though only entering squadron service in January 1943, had become the standard fast carrier fighter by August of that year. With their Corsairs and Hellcats, the American naval airmen at last had machines superior to Japan's redoubtable Zeros.

Yet it would be grossly unjust to suggest that the American triumphs in 1943 and 1944 resulted only from superiority in numbers and in technology. It should not be forgotten that they had enjoyed several advantages during the Guadalcanal campaign, notably their SG radar sets and their foreknowledge of the enemy's plans as a result of their ability to break his codes. However, these had not saved them from defeat even on occasions when their forces had also been more powerful, as at Savo Island, or much more powerful, as at Tassafaronga.

The reasons for these defeats were basic. The Japanese seamen and airmen were highly trained, highly experienced and well-practised in the tactics they would be called upon to employ. The American ships and squadrons on the contrary contained a high proportion of new recruits who had entered the service only after the commencement of hostilities and who were sent into action in hastily improvised units, after the barest minimum of training, with little knowledge of the problems likely to confront them. In a word, the Japanese were professional; the Americans (with only a few exceptions) were amateurs.

It was not until the Guadalcanal campaign that this situation changed. In that campaign, the Japanese lost not only vital ships and aeroplanes but many of their finest men. This was especially the case with regard to their Naval Air Force. Sometimes the casualties occurred in one furious action as when the dive-bomber and torpedo-plane commanders were killed at Santa Cruz. On other occasions they resulted from attrition. The enemy's finest fighter unit at the start of the campaign was undoubtedly the Tainan Air Group. By November, it had been forced to return to Japan having been almost annihilated. Its best pilot, Petty Officer Sakai, as described earlier, was critically wounded on the very first day's fighting on 7th August. His successor as the unit's top-scorer, Petty Officer Ota, died in action

---

* However, in the Royal Navy, which was desperately short of modern equipment, the Corsair first went into action afloat in April 1944.

over Guadalcanal on 21st October. Their commander, Lieutenant Sasai, was killed on 26th August.

It proved impossible to replace such men. Among other essential items, Japan was short of aviation fuel. In consequence, the amount of training that could be given to new recruits was vastly reduced. At the start of the war, most Japanese airmen had between 500 and 800 hours flying experience, often gained in the fighting in China. In 1943, the average pilot, on joining an operational Air Group, had only 50 to 100 hours experience. The Americans were not so restricted; their airmen had flown at least 600 hours prior to engaging in combat.

The resulting decline in the quality of Japanese fighter pilots was already evident before the end of the Guadalcanal campaign. In September, the Americans were still being warned that it was 'suicide' to attempt to 'dog-fight' with a Zero, yet by the end of October, the Wildcats of 'Cactus Air Force' were not only doing this but were enjoying considerable success. By the time of the attacks on the enemy reinforcement convoy on 14th November, it was the Zeros that were reluctant to engage the Wildcats.

The decline of the Japanese bomber pilots perhaps became really apparent only in April 1943. The enemy had mustered some 300 aircraft in New Britain, including 170 transferred from the Japanese carriers. On 7th April, 67 Vals, escorted by 120 Zeros, attacked shipping in Ironbottom Sound. They achieved meagre results, sinking destroyer *Aaron Ward*, a survivor of Callaghan's night action, tanker *Kanawha* and the New Zealand minesweeper *Moa*, which had helped to destroy *I-1*; but losing twelve dive-bombers and nine Zeros. Seven American fighters were also lost but all the pilots except one survived.

Later attacks in similar strength on bases in New Guinea resulted in further casualties but even less success. Their only long-term effect was another reduction in the numbers of Japan"s front-line airmen. A few days after the last raid, the Americans, as already described, gave the final proof of their dominance in the air by killing the Imperial Navy's Commander-in-Chief, who, incidentally, had wished to inspect installations and raise morale in preparation for further air-strikes. These were later carried out by his successors. They followed a depressing pattern : ever-diminishing results at a cost of ever-growing losses.

Even in the night surface-actions where the Americans had been at their worst, they had now learned almost all the necessary lessons. Kinkaid's proposals might have been ignored at Tassafaronga but, in the words of Nimitz, they 'pointed the way toward better night tactics'. Tanaka would later admit that as a result of its experiences, the United States Navy 'grew wise'. By the end of the Guadalcanal campaign, the Americans had in practice taken the final step needed to defeat their foes; they had become professionals as well.

So the death of Yamamoto proved doubly symbolic. Not only was Operation 'Vengeance' mounted from Guadalcanal to kill the Admiral but as a result of the lessons learned at Guadalcanal, the United States Navy was able to gain revenge for all previous misfortunes.

For the remainder of 1943, the Americans proceeded with the conquest of the central and northern Solomons, fighting a series of night actions which gradually brought greater success as they became more practised in their newly-learned techniques, particularly the independent use of destroyers that Kinkaid had advocated. Then in 1944, with the benefit of the massive new carrier force that they had built up in the previous year, they began taking giant strides towards the heart of the Japanese domains, isolating and reducing to impotence such powerful bases as Rabaul and Truk. The process culminated on 19th–20th June, in the Battle of the Philippine Sea, when the Japanese lost three carriers (including the veteran *Shokaku*) and almost all their remaining carrier-based airmen.

In consequence, when the great fleet action of which Yamamoto had once dreamed, at last took place, it was fought not to complete Japan's triumph but as a desperate attempt to prevent the American re-conquest of the Philippines which would finally sever the supply-lines to Japan's conquests in the south. The Battle of Leyte Gulf lasted from 23rd to 26th October 1944. When it was over, the American Third Fleet – commanded by Halsey – and the American Seventh Fleet – commanded by Kinkaid – had lost a total of one light carrier, two escort carriers, two destroyers and one destroyer-escort. The Japanese losses: fleet carrier *Zuikaku*; light carriers *Zuiho*, *Chitose* and her sister-ship *Chiyoda*; three battleships; six heavy cruisers (including *Chokai* which had carried Mikawa's flag at Savo Island); four light cruisers; nine destroyers.

During the course of the fighting, there had been strikes by carriers, surface-actions in daylight and surface-actions at night. In all of these the Americans had proved superior, despite the fact that at one crucial moment in the battle, their forces were very heavily outnumbered at the scene of combat. Perhaps, after all, Yamamoto had been lucky not to live long enough to see the ruin of his beloved Navy.

The series of successes which culminated in this overwhelming victory was gained as a result of the Americans' experiences in the brutal actions in the southern Solomons during the last five months of 1942. It was from these that they developed the skills necessary for their advance across the Pacific. The final judgement may well be that of their most resolute opponent in those actions. 'There is no question,' said Raizo Tanaka, 'that Japan's doom was sealed with the closing of the struggle for Guadalcanal.'

GUADALCANAL

No man who fought in those bloody waters can forget the apprehension, the exultation and the terror that he experienced, the hideous forms of death that he witnessed, or the self-sacrificing heroism that gave him a new respect for his fellow seamen. 'Savo', 'Guadalcanal', 'Tassafaronga' and the rest are no mere battle names to the survivors; they are flaming banners of deathless deeds by ships and men whose bones forever rest in Ironbottom Sound.

So, reader, if this tale has seemed repetitious with shock and gore, exploding magazines, burning and sinking ships and plummeting planes – that is simply how it was.

> – Samuel Eliot Morison:
> *History of United States Naval Operations in World War II*,
> Vol V 'The Struggle for Guadalcanal'.

Bibliography and Acknowledgements

Bibliography

Bennett, Geoffrey: *Naval Battles of World War II*. Batsford 1975.

Brown, David: *Carrier Fighters*, Macdonalds & Janes 1975. ᴏɴᴇ ᴏꜰ ᴛʜᴇ ʙᴇꜱᴛ

Costello, John: *The Pacific War*, Collins 1981.

D'Albas, Andrieu: *Death of a Navy*, Robert Hale Ltd. 1957.

Dull, Paul S.: *A Battle History of the Imperial Japanese Navy (1941–1945)*, Patrick Stephens Ltd, Cambridge 1978.

Fuller, Major-General J. F. C.: *The Second World War (1939–1945)* Eyre & Spottiswoode 1948 (Revised 1954).

Griffith, Brigadier General Samuel B, USMC: *The Battle for Guadalcanal*, The Nautical & Aviation Publishing Company of America 1979.

Hough, Major Frank: *The Island War*, J. B. Lippincott & Co, Philadelphia 1947.

Howarth, Stephen: *Morning Glory: A History of the Imperial Japanese Navy*, Hamish Hamilton 1983.

Kahn, David: *The Codebreakers*, Weidenfeld & Nicolson 1973.

Killen, John: *A History of Marine Aviation 1911–68*, Frederick Muller 1969.

Lewin, Ronald: *The Other Ultra*, Hutchinson 1982.

Liddell Hart, B. H.: *History of the Second World War*, Cassell 1970.

Lord, Walter: *Lonely Vigil: Coastwatchers of the Solomons*, Allen Lane 1978.

MacArthur, General Douglas: *Reminiscences*, William Heinemann Ltd. 1964.

MacIntyre, Captain Donald: *The Battle for the Pacific*, Batsford 1966.

MacIntyre, Captain Donald: *The Thunder of the Guns*, Frederick Muller Ltd. 1959.

MacIntyre, Captain Donald: *Wings of Neptune: The story of Naval Aviation*, Peter Davies 1963.

Miller, Thomas G.: *The Cactus Air Force: The story of the Handful of Fliers who Saved Guadalcanal*, Harper & Row 1969.

Morison, Samuel Eliot: *History of United States Naval Operations in World War II*, Little Brown & Co.:—

Volume IV: *Coral Sea, Midway & Submarine Actions May 1942– August 1942*, 1948 (Includes account of the landings on Guadalcanal & Tulagi).

Volume V: *The Struggle for Guadalcanal, August 1942–February 1943*, 1949.

Morison, Samuel Eliot: *The Two-Ocean War: A Short History of the United States Navy in the Second World War*, Little Brown & Co. 1965 (This is not only a summary of but an up-dating of his earlier history).

Newcomb, Richard F.: *Savo: The Incredible Naval Debacle off Guadalcanal*, Holt Rinehart & Winston, New York 1961.

Okumiya, Masatake & Horikoshi, Jiro with Caidin, Martin: *Zero!*, Cassell 1957.

Potter, E. B. & Nimitz, Fleet Admiral Chester W.: *The Great Sea War*, George G. Harrap & Co. Ltd. 1961.

Purnell's *History of the Second World War*. Articles:

Roetter, Charles: 'Guadalcanal: The Land Battles';

MacIntyre, Captain Donald: 'Guadalcanal: The Sea Battles';

MacIntyre, Captain Donald: 'Guadalcanal: The Final Actions';

Kennedy, Paul: 'Zenith of the Rising Sun'.

Roskill, Captain S. W.: *The War at Sea* (Volume II), HMSO 1956.

Ruge, Vice-Admiral Friedrich: *Sea Warfare 1939–1945: A German Viewpoint*, Cassell 1957. (Includes also accounts of the actions in the Pacific from a Japanese viewpoint).

Sakai, Saburo: *Samurai*, Kimbers 1959.

Shores, Christopher: *Air Aces*, Bison Books 1983.

Tanaka, Rear-Admiral Raizo with Pineau, Roger: *Japan's Losing Struggle for Guadalcanal*, United States Naval Institute Proceedings, 1956.

Van der Rhoer, Edward: *Deadly Magic*, Charles Scribners' Sons 1978.

Acknowledgements

My thanks are due to The Nautical and Aviation Publishing Company of Baltimore for permission to reproduce a passage from *The Battle for Guadalcanal* by Brigadier-General Samuel B. Griffith and to Little Brown & Co., Boston, for permission to quote a passage from *The Two Ocean War* by Samuel Eliot Morison.

Material some of which has not been published was also kindly made available by Mr Chaz Bowyer, Mr Christopher Shores and the Staffs of the Air Historical and Naval Historical Branches of the Ministry of Defence, especially Mr David Brown of the Naval Historical Branch who also read the manuscript and suggested numerous improvements thereto. To all of them also my thanks.

Index

Index